your **dog** IQ

your **dog's IQ**

How clever is your canine?

David Taylor

THUNDER BAY
P · R · E · S · S
San Diego, California

Thunder Bay Press
An imprint of the Advantage Publishers Group
THUNDER BAY   10350 Barnes Canyon Road, San Diego, CA 92121
P · R · E · S · S   www.thunderbaybooks.com

All notations of errors or omissions should be
addressed to Thunder Bay Press, Editorial
Department,at the above address. All other
correspondence (author inquiries,
permissions) concerning the content of this
book should be addressed to
Octopus Publishing Group
2–4 Heron Quays, London E14 4JP

ISBN-13: 978-1-59223-987-0
ISBN-10: 1-59223-987-0

Library of Congress Cataloging-in-Publication Data
Taylor, David, 1934-
   Your dog's IQ : how clever is your canine? / David Taylor.
      p. cm. Includes index.
   ISBN-13: 978-1-59223-987-0
   ISBN-10: 1-59223-987-0
   1. Dogs--Psychology. 2. Dogs--Training. I. Title.
   SF433.T393 2009
   636.7--dc22
                        2008045830

Printed and bound in China
1 2 3 4 5 13 12 11 10 09

Contents

Introduction

We all want to believe the best about those we love. In the case of our kids, we like to think they are smart, and examinations and parent/teacher meetings can provide the evidence for our children's abilities. But what about our dogs?

Do the apparently clever things dogs occasionally do really prove that they are intelligent? Is one dog more intelligent than another? And what exactly do we mean by the word "intelligence" when it is applied to our pets?

All these questions and more are considered in this book. The tests described will lead you to some interesting conclusions about the thinking power of your dog, and by repeating them and perhaps reinforcing certain aspects of training you will actually be able to improve his IQ—whether he is a pedigree show champion or a mongrel from the local rescue center.

Most of the tests are simple to set up and many can conveniently be carried out when you take your dog for his regular walk or during play sessions indoors or out. Who knows—your family pet may surprise you and turn out to be a canine mastermind!

the canine
mind

How brainy is your dog?

The brain power of a dog is difficult to measure. However, you will know from experience that your pet constantly displays his intelligence in a wide variety of circumstances—and not just by quickly learning how to open the refrigerator door when there's a freshly cooked chicken inside!

Does brain size matter?

A dog's reasoning power lags far behind that of a human being and he lacks our ability to associate complicated, abstract ideas. However, it is not clear whether this is directly related to brain size.

While the human brain weighs around 3 pounds, a dog such as the Beagle can muster only 2¹/₂ ounces. Although it was once considered that the bigger the brain (as a proportion of body weight) the greater the intelligence—since larger brains possess more nerve connections—very recent research has come to the conclusion that this is not true (see also pages 12–13). Big dogs carrying bigger brains are not necessarily more intelligent than breeds with smaller ones.

The human–canine relationship

According to behavioral scientists, dogs don't make the top ten list of most intelligent animals—they are even less intelligent than pigs! However, dogs were the first animals to be domesticated by man purely because of their versatile abilities.

By selective breeding across millennia, specialized breeds of dog have been developed to be expert in particular types of work. That is why, when you talk to your neighbor about how bright your spaniel is, he will claim an equally high IQ for his poodle. The two breeds have developed different talents, within a genus common to both for friendship, cooperation, and mutual understanding between owner and dog.

So, whether or not pigs are more intelligent than dogs, can you really picture a pig playing hide-and-seek with the kids, fetching the newspaper, guiding a blind person, or cuddling up on the lap of a retiree living alone? I certainly cannot.

Your dog's brain

For an animal of his size, the frontal lobes of a dog's brain are relatively large, although nothing like as large as a human's. It is here that the most highly developed sectors of mental activity are located: consciousness, the power of thought, and intellect.

Growing intelligence

As with other animals, a dog's brain continues to grow after birth. The number of connections between brain cells multiplies as the dog's senses receive an ever-increasing number of stimuli from the world around him. This may be the major reason why mutts, which are generally more streetwise than purebreds, tend to have bigger brains than their pedigree relatives.

Mental exercise

As a consequence of all this, you can expect your dog to become brighter the more he learns, the more challenges he has to face, and the more problems he needs to solve. Just like muscles that develop through working out in the gym, the brain of a young dog increases in size and that of an older dog functions much better with exercise.

The games, tests, and training in this book can act as a mental gymnasium for your pet. In addition, the physical exercise your dog receives when playing these games also benefits his brain, by the heart pumping plenty of blood to bring vital oxygen and nourishment in the form of sugars, proteins, and vitamins to the thinking cells. Insufficient exercise can lead to deficiencies in the nutrition of a dog's brain cells and may play a part in the development of Canine Cognitive Dysfunction (CCD), with its associated weakening of mental powers in older pets (see pages 180–181).

Canine reasoning

Dogs are skilled problem solvers and their owners play an important part in developing this talent. Scientists have found that many dogs are very good at imitating people and learning from them.

Living with people

Dogs have evolved an innate ability to watch, communicate with, and work alongside people. Their wild relatives, the wolves, cannot do this. For example, a wolf will unlock a gate after watching a human do it but a dog will not—until he is given permission to do so by his owner (at least in theory). Dogs live within and come to understand the rules of human society.

Complex reasoning

Unlike many other animals, dogs reason in quite sophisticated ways. If a food treat is put in a hole and the opening is covered with a cloth, then apes, monkeys, cats, hamsters, parrots, and dogs will all go and retrieve it. Having watched the food being hidden under the cloth, the animal does not need to carry a mental image of it in his brain.

If, on the other hand, the food is placed under a cup that is then slid behind one of two screens and the food then removed before showing the empty cup to the animal, he must calculate that the food has been deposited behind one of the screens when out of his sight.

To reason like this and then successfully retrieve the food, the animal must retain an image of the food in his mind. Dogs, some apes, and monkeys can do this while cats, hamsters, and parrots cannot.

Recently, scientists have thrown some doubt on dogs' successful performance in such tests. When tighter controls were introduced to a similar test where food or a toy was transferred from a small container into one of three boxes, the dogs simply went to the box closest to the small container.

We can only conclude that although not even close to that of human beings, dogs' reasoning ability is well developed in comparison to that of most other mammals.

Comparative intelligence

Comparing intelligence between individuals of different species is extraordinarily difficult, if not impossible. For example, dolphins perform amazing feats in their watery world, but how do you even begin to formulate a test to compare their intelligence with that of, say, a sheepdog on an alpine farm?

Closer comparisons?

It would even be difficult to compare the dog with other terrestrial species, such as the chimpanzee or the horse. The chimpanzee has the enormous advantage of hands with opposable thumbs and can use tools, while dogs patently cannot. Horses are intelligent prey animals, whose talents lie in defending themselves efficiently in various ways against attackers, whereas the dog has developed his skills as a pack-hunting predator.

Brain capacity

Some scientists have tried to use an empirical approach to the question of comparative intelligence. This involves calculating the amount of brain tissue that is additional to what is needed to control basic bodily functions like breathing, blood circulation, movement, and so on. This "excess brain capacity" is available for the animal to gain more information about the world via his senses and to go on to think, imagine, and "be intelligent" by processing these pieces of data.

The amount of this "excess" is calculated by comparing the weight of the brain to the length of the spinal cord (which controls all the basic bodily functions), to give a ratio that should be greater in the more intelligent species. Results show an average of:

- Humans 50:1
- Dogs 5:1
- Cats 4:1

Comparing the weight of the brain to the length of the spinal cord is the best *physical* method of estimating intelligence but is far from perfect.

Breed intelligence

It may be difficult to compare the intelligence of different species (see pages 16–17), but is it possible to make a meaningful comparison between the various breeds of dog?

Aspects of intelligence

Three types of canine intelligence have been identified:

1. Adaptive Ability to learn and solve problems.

2. Obedient Ability and readiness to respond appropriately to commands.

3. Instinctive Inherited ability to do certain kinds of work, such as herding or retrieving.

The tests in this book address all three types, but particularly the first two.

Judging intelligence

One study asked dog obedience judges which breeds were the most trainable and how quickly they learned new commands. The most intelligent breeds needed fewer than five repetitions to understand a new command, and obeyed a first command 95 percent of the time or more; the least intelligent needed 80 repetitions or more and obeyed 25 percent of the time or less.

Does this matter? The "least intelligent" bunch contains dogs that can be as loving, sociable, and entertaining as any other. Personality certainly plays its part (see pages 28–29), and breeders of such dogs often insist they *are* bright but simply don't obey human commands due to their independent spirit.

Mutt intelligence

Many mutts are extremely smart. They benefit from their "hybrid vigor": the increased strength of some characteristics in hybrids due to a combination of the "virtues" of their parents and more distant forebears.

Most intelligent	Least intelligent
Australian cattle dog	Afghan hound
border collie	basenji
Doberman pinscher	basset hound
German shepherd	beagle
Labrador retriever	bloodhound
papillon	borzoi
poodle	bulldog
rottweiler	chow chow
Shetland sheepdog	mastiff
	Pekingese
	shih tzu

Afghan hound

canine
thought

How clever can dogs be?

Intellect is the capacity for understanding, thinking, and reasoning, as distinct from feeling or wishing. Dogs certainly possess intellect and they use it, often quite remarkably, to solve problems.

Two very smart dogs

There is plenty of anecdotal evidence to support the idea that dogs can sometimes display remarkable powers of thought.

Spatial awareness

One particular German shepherd loved to retrieve sticks thrown for him. When his owner threw a small branch over the garden fence, which was built of vertical wooden planks, the dog dashed through a gap where a single plank was missing to collect it. Seizing the branch in his jaws, he began to trot back towards the garden. As he approached, he evidently realized that with the branch held horizontally between his teeth he would not be able to run straight through the gap so, still trotting, he turned his head to one side until the branch was vertical and slipped through into the garden with ease.

Vet alarm

A working border collie spent his days out in the fields keeping an eye on his owner's herd of cattle. This dog understood the normal behavior of cows in detail, and was very quick to spot anything that was slightly odd about their demeanor. For example, the moment he saw a cow not lying comfortably at rest but with stiffly extended limbs—a sign of so-called "milk fever"—he would at once dash to the farmhouse to raise the alarm, allowing the vet to be called in good time. He never once sent either farmer or vet on a wild goose chase. That dog really knew each one of the cows in his care.

Canine senses

A dog's overall intelligence relies first of all on the gathering of information from the world around him. He does this via his formidable array of senses, which include sight, smell, and hearing. These canine senses are quite different in intensity to our own, so require some explanation.

Sight

Although most dog breeds do not hunt primarily by sight, canine vision is well adapted to tracking small, fast-moving prey. Their eyes are not sensitive to color, but have a wider visual field than our own. Dogs also see much better in the dark, due to a retina that is dominated by cells, called rods, that are sensitive to low light, and a shiny layer of cells beneath the rods, called the *tapetum lucidum*, which reflects light back through them.

Smell

It is well known that dogs have a wonderful sense of smell—in fact, it is about one million times more sensitive than our own. We have about five million smell-sensing cells in our noses: dachshunds, for example, have 125 million and German shepherds 220 million. In the rest of the animal kingdom, only eels and butterflies smell as efficiently as dogs.

Hearing

Hearing is something else at which dogs excel. They can register sounds of 35,000 vibrations per second, compared to 25,000 for cats, and 20,000 for humans. They are also sensitive enough to tell the difference between (for example) two metronomes, one ticking at 100 beats per minute and the other at 96—which we cannot.

Super senses

One of our senses is better than that of our dogs: taste. Dogs' ancestors were carnivores, spotting their prey at a distance and eating whatever they could catch, whereas ours were omnivores, selecting from a range of different-tasting foods. However, dogs do possess a variety of other sensitivities that we do not.

Vibrations

Dogs are very sensitive to vibrations, enabling them to give warning of earthquakes and volcanic eruptions some considerable time before we become aware of any movement. Curiously, they only react like this to the imminence of true earthquakes and ignore the 150,000 other harmless vibrations of the earth's crust that occur each year.

Medical help

Some dogs have the curious ability to detect an oncoming epileptic fit in a person well before it occurs. Others give warning of dangerous rises in their owners' blood pressure. We don't yet know how they do this, although it may be that they spot very faint warning symptoms in the patient via their highly developed powers of observation.

Sixth sense?

According to surveys, 48 percent of dog owners in the United States and United Kingdom believe their pets to be telepathic. However, the familiar reports of dogs knowing when their owner is on the way home, or when they themselves are about to be taken to the vet clinic or for a walk, can be explained without it. For example, the dogs' acute senses may detect the sound of a familiar car, and an owner's preparatory behavior when planning a clinic visit or walk are quickly picked up by these highly perceptive animals.

Personality

The thinking processes of dogs are complex and different from those of, say, cats or horses. In many respects, they resemble those of humans: hardly surprising when they have watched, copied, remembered, and learned from our ways over millennia. A dog's intellect is also molded by inherited factors, and through social contacts that should begin early in life.

Your pet is unique

Each dog, whatever his pedigree, is an individual with his own distinct personality. Even within the same breed, dogs' characters vary greatly.

Some of the most interesting canine characters can be found among the mutts: they have the great advantage of inheriting genes from a wider pool than pedigrees and consequently their personalities can display the strong points of each breed in their makeup, while diminishing the sometimes undesirable traits of many purebreds. Crossbred dogs are often tougher, better tempered, and more adaptable than their pedigree counterparts. They also tend to be less disease-prone.

Character assessment

A dog's personality can be assessed by conducting tests that were originally applied to humans. First, the owner is asked to rate their pet on four aspects of personality:

1. Energetic–slothful
2. Affectionate–aggressive
3. Calm-anxious
4. Intelligent-stupid

Next, total strangers rate the animal according to the same characteristics by noting his behavior during tests for the four trait couples. For example, intelligence—or a lack thereof—can be judged by the animal's ability to retrieve a treat (see pages 66–67). Consistently, the strangers' assessments correlate with what owners say about their pets, eliminating any tendency an owner might have to exaggerate the favorable points of their pet's personality.

Wishful thinking?

We all like to imagine—or even firmly believe—that our dogs are energetic, affectionate, calm, and intelligent. Whatever the truth, the tests, games, and training in this book can help your dog to become more like the (perhaps idealized!) picture you have of him.

Emotions

Dogs appear to possess emotional intelligence: they are able to love, hate, and grieve. Their love and loyalty are unconditional—much like that between parent and child—and some animal psychologists believe these emotions are instinctive rather than developed as a result of the dog's life experiences. It is, however, impossible to prove that canine emotions are innate.

People prejudice

Dogs can be prejudiced and may show dislike or even aggression toward people of a certain appearance. However, such prejudice is not inherent in the animal but may be the result of a bad experience in the past or, because the dog feels himself to be part of his human family (see pages 32–33), by him picking up and copying any antipathy shown by his owner toward particular individuals.

Dogs of war

Throughout history, in some parts of the world war dogs have been trained to recognize the physical characteristics and typical dress of enemy troops and then attack them. Attila the Hun used giant Molossian dogs, precursors of the mastiff, and Talbots, ancestors of the bloodhound, for this purpose as his armies swept across Europe.

Bobby's grief

One of the most famous examples of canine grief is that of Greyfriars Bobby, a Skye terrier who lived in Edinburgh. In 1858, after his master's death, Bobby followed the coffin to the churchyard and attended the ceremony, defying all efforts to send him on his way. The little dog spent the following fourteen years until his own death living around the churchyard, apparently grieving for his lost friend and master.

Pack reasoning

In countries where the front doors of houses are commonly
fitted with mailboxes, the classic dog-versus-postman scenario is
not an example of irrational canine prejudice but rather the
product of logical reasoning.

The family pack

The domestic dog is a member of a pack: the family household. Unknown
human or canine individuals are initially viewed with suspicion and the
territory is protected. If a stranger is accepted without aggression by a
family member, they will normally also be accepted by the dog.

A cowardly intruder

Now let's look at the familiar scene of the postman arriving at the door,
from the dog's point of view:

- Up the path walks a stranger, the postman. No family member comes
  out to greet him.
- The dog therefore warns off the postman by barking.
- After fumbling at the door and failing to enter, the postman retreats.
- The dog is triumphant—it took merely a bark or two for the coward to
  run away!
- Each day, "intruder" and dog go through the same performance.
- Before long, the dog comes to consider the postman's uniform as the
  mark of a coward who can be chased and expected to retreat.

Throughout, the dog has acted rationally and confidently as a member of
the family pack, protecting the pack's territory.

Mailbox mayhem

In countries where the postman deposits letters in a mailbox at the gates of the property, a pet dog given the run of the garden will reach the same conclusion: here is a cowardly person who does not enter the family pack territory and retreats in fear every day, apparently in response to just a bark or two.

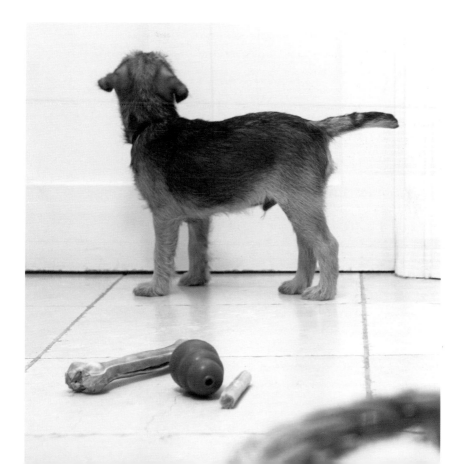

Some clever canines

There are innumerable examples of dogs doing a wide variety of clever things that illustrate their undoubted intelligence. For example, accounts appear quite regularly in the media of people being saved from house fires or gas escapes through a warning given by their pets. As in the incidents described on this and the following pages, we cannot doubt that dogs' affinity with and love for their human friends lies behind these displays of intelligence, courage, and resourcefulness.

Titanic effort

In one league table of 100 breeds compiled according to their intelligence, Newfoundlands appear quite low down, at 34. Yet it was a Newfoundland that saved Napoleon Bonaparte from drowning, and another that in 1912 led one of the doomed *Titanic's* lifeboats to safety after the ship had collided with an iceberg.

Rigel belonged to the First Officer of the *Titanic*. As the ship began to sink, he plunged into the sea and guided one of the lifeboats towards the *Carpathia*, the first ship to reach the stricken vessel. Suddenly, the lifeboat began to drift perilously under the *Carpathia's* bows, its huddled cargo of survivors too weak and shocked to shout a warning. Swimming ahead, the dog saw the danger and began barking repeatedly to attract the attention of the ship's bridge. Its captain heard the barking, spotted the lifeboat, and immediately stopped all engines. Everyone in the lifeboat, as well as Rigel—who by now had been paddling valiantly for three hours in the ice-cold water—was saved.

Scotland to India . . . and back

Still on the subject of sea voyages, a lady dog owner from Inverness in Scotland sent her border collie to live with a friend in Calcutta, India.

Some months later, the dog suddenly turned up again at his old home in Inverness! He had apparently boarded a ship in Calcutta that was bound for Dundee, and once there had transferred to a coastal vessel sailing to Inverness. It was rumored that the dog had been attracted by the familiar Scottish accents of crew members on both ships.

Pure gold

Dorado, a four-year-old Labrador, became caught up in the horrific events of 9/11 in New York. He was the guide dog of a blind computer technician, Omar Rivera, who was working on the seventy-first floor of the World Trade Center's north tower when the hijacked aircraft struck the building above him. Here is how Mr. Rivera described what happened next:

"I stood up and I could hear how pieces of glass were flying around and falling. I could feel the smoke filling my lungs and the heat was unbearable. Not having any sight I knew I wouldn't be able to run down the stairs and through all the obstacles like other people. I was resigned to dying and decided to free Dorado to give him a chance of escape, so I unclipped his lead, ruffled his head, gave him a nudge and ordered him to go."

At that moment Dorado was swept away by the rush of panicking people fleeing down the stairs and Mr. Rivera found himself alone amid the chaos for several minutes. But then the unexpected happened: he found himself nudged at knee-height in a familiar, fuzzy-muzzled way. Dorado had come back for his master.

The dog proceeded to guide Mr. Rivera down seventy flights of stairs, the stairwell packed with shoving, pushing, terrified folk. It took more than an hour, with Dorado nudging his friend down step by step, for the pair to reach ground level and safety. Not long after they did so, the tower collapsed. Dorado certainly lived up to his name, which means "golden" and provides a supreme example of canine intelligence, including emotional intelligence.

Canine navigation

Another example of the cleverness of dogs is their ability to navigate over long distances when finding their way home. In 1923 one of the most famous canine trekkers, a border collie named Bobbie, later dubbed the Wonder Dog of Oregon, covered 2,550 miles in returning to his home in Silverton, Oregon. His owners had taken him on a trip to Indiana in the Midwest and he had taken it upon himself to navigate his way home. The townsfolk of Silverton still celebrate his return.

How does a dog achieve such an amazing feat? The truth is we do not know for sure. Possibilities include:

Celestial navigation The dog may subconsciously note the angle of the sun at a certain time of day and then compare it with the angle it would be at the same time over his home. Noting a difference, the dog might then move in a particular direction, check the sun again, and, finding the angle "worse," change course. When the angle improves, this indicates the "correct" direction. But how can the dog know what time it is? It seems probable that, in common with man and the higher mammals (and, incidentally, cockroaches) dogs possess an internal biological clock.

Internal compass It is also possible that like pigeons, bees, dolphins, cattle, and many other animals, dogs use crystals of the naturally magnetic iron compound, magnetite, to help them respond to the position and intensity of the earth's magnetic field. Such crystals in the brains of dogs may well act as compasses. How exactly such a compass works within brain cells has yet to be determined but it probably acts as a direction finder in conjunction with the dog's ability in celestial navigation described above.

Cognitive mapping Over much shorter distances, dogs find their way home using a cognitive map of the home range area that they have stored in their brains during all their previous wanderings. This map contains a record of how key points in the environment are related geometrically, and so enables the dog to take the shortest route home once he has located the target destination. Old dogs suffering from the condition of Canine Cognitive Dysfunction tend to get lost when wandering around the neighborhood. The cognitive maps of their home range area have faded from their brains.

testing aims and scoring

Fair tests for all breeds

It is difficult to set up intelligence tests that are equally fair to all types of dog. For example, sight hounds such as greyhounds and salukis would obviously outperform scent hounds such as bloodhounds and dachshunds in tests involving visual clues, and vice versa.

Contrasting abilities

The beagle, a fine hunter, displays an intelligence when working out in the field that would not be appropriate in, say, a border collie or Australian cattle dog.

The beagle concentrates intently on picking up and then following a scent trail to its source, and will ignore all distractions other than the commands of his handler. By contrast, a border collie working a flock of sheep must be able to juggle multiple incoming perceptions at the same time, including distractions. He must keep the sheep moving in the right direction, at the right speed, as a fairly compact mass. He must keep an eye open for stragglers, dawdlers, or fugitives, and scan the surrounding area for any sign of danger or difficulty, all the while remaining alert to respond to any signal from the shepherd.

Border collies may be highly intelligent, but a potential downside of their sharp-wittedness is their ability to learn things that their owners would rather they did not know, and get into trouble easily when boredom sets in.

Physical differences

The physical characteristics of a dog are clearly important when devising fair tests: his overall size and build, any special anatomical features of his breed, his age, and, of course, the presence of any physical disability such as those affecting vision, hearing, or locomotion.

The IQ tests

In this book I have aimed to balance the range of tests as fairly as possible, so that no single type of dog has an advantage over the others. Working breeds, toy dogs, talented sniffers, and sharp-eyed hunters will all be on a roughly equal footing overall.

The tests in this book are great fun for both dog and owner, and should be regarded as games—which, indeed, most of them are. Little is required in the way of equipment, and none of the tests is particularly time consuming. They aim to demonstrate various different aspects of your dog's intelligence: his powers of analysis and problem solving, and his ability to make mental connections.

Scoring the tests

A scoring system is provided for each test. Add up the scores for the tests in each section as you and your dog complete them, then compute the grand total at the end. Spread the testing period over as many days or weeks as you wish. You can omit some tests if you prefer, although this will affect your dog's grand total.

Test and train

If your dog achieves better scores in some sections than others on first testing, concentrate on his weaker performances and increase the number of testings in that section. At the same time, mix in regular training sessions (see pages 152–177).

There's no rush

Do not begin IQ testing your dog until he:

- Is at least one year old.
- Has known you for at least six months.
- Has lived in your home, where some of the tests will be carried out, for a minimum of two months.

Is my dog stupid?

Many dogs that are really quite intelligent give the opposite impression because they are easily distracted. This tendency is often seen in more lively, inquisitive little dogs like terriers. They find the world around them so interesting that it is difficult for them to concentrate on anything for too long.

Bonus scores

On pages 138–139 you will find bonus points to be added to the grand total according to your dog's breed. These are based on the fact that the selective development of breeds has altered the ways in which each best displays its intelligence.

Keep it fun!

Don't take these tests too seriously, and do avoid bragging about your dog's grand total at your local training class. Your pet is a loyal, loving, amusing, cooperative, fascinating, and useful family member. If *you* consider him to be smart, he is; if you don't, you still know him to be the finest dog in the world! Most importantly, keep telling him he is. Give plenty of praise when praise is due.

the IQ tests

Introduction to the tests

The tests begin on page 50 and are divided into six sections, each covering a different aspect of canine intelligence. These are: problem solving, analytical powers, general IQ, memory and observation, mental linkage, and life experience.

Improving your dog's score

In the first test series you carry out, perform each test only once: if you keep repeating a test, it becomes a form of training.

When you have completed all the tests and arrived at your dog's grand total score, you can then repeat the series, preferably after your pet has undergone some extra teaching (see pages 152–177). With any luck, your dog will then hit a higher score—and *that* will be the one you tell your neighbor about!

You can—and should—continue to challenge your dog regularly with a test or two, both for the fun of it and as a sure way to continue developing his intelligence.

Working together

The tests work best when there is a close relationship between you and your dog, particularly if he is already obedience trained.

It is best to test when:

• Your dog will not be distracted by the presence of other animals or people, particularly children, creating some disturbance nearby.

Using food treats

The test instructions make frequent reference to rewarding your dog with food treats. These should be small and easy to handle. Good choices are your pet's favorite dog biscuits and cubes of hard cheese. Do **not** give sweets or chocolates as treats, as they may contain substances that are toxic to dogs (see pages 154–157).

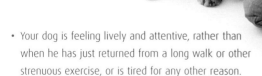

- Your dog is feeling lively and attentive, rather than when he has just returned from a long walk or other strenuous exercise, or is tired for any other reason.
- You, too, are feeling fresh and ready to oversee the tests properly.

Section A
Problem-solving tests

To solve a problem with which he is faced, your dog has to combine several aspects of his intelligence. This will vary according to the nature of the test: analytical ability, use of senses (particularly visual observation), memory, and general intelligence will all be in the mix. Consequently, tests in this section will overlap with some of those in other sections.

Top problem solvers

Pastoral breeds such as the border collie and German shepherd are especially good at working out solutions to problems. They don't simply perform single tasks under the supervision of their owner, such as guarding premises or pulling a load, but are accustomed to being self-reliant and resourceful when out working alone with their owner some distance away. They love the challenge of a real job and for this reason such dogs are not generally very happy when kept purely as house pets.

Learning to solve problems

Although much of a dog's problem-solving ability is innate, training and experience are also vital in developing it. Collies have to learn the ways of sheep and cattle, as well as how to interpret a shepherd's or farmer's instructions delivered by voice, whistle, or gesture. It is the same for your pet. Basic and, later, specific training carried out regularly by you (see pages 152–177) is necessary to enhance your dog's ability to demonstrate intelligent behavior. As with the collie out rounding up a flock on the hillside, your pet will thoroughly enjoy it—and, hopefully, so will you.

1. Houdini hound

This is a good first test, which entails your dog analyzing his situation and then doing something about it. How quickly can your pet solve the problem?

You will need:
- Large bath towel
- Stopwatch, or wristwatch with a second hand

What to do

1. With your dog up and about, let him sniff and visually inspect the towel.
2. With a swift, smooth motion, throw the towel over your dog to cover his head and neck completely.
3. Start timing, but remain completely silent: no words of encouragement, please. See how long it takes for your pet to free himself.

What's his score?

5 points if your dog frees himself in less than 5 seconds.

4 points if he frees himself in 5–15 seconds.

3 points if he frees himself in 15–30 seconds.

2 points if he frees himself in 30–60 seconds.

0 points if he takes more than 60 seconds to free himself.

Do not be despondent if your dog sits there with the towel on his head for minute after minute. I once had a very bright West Highland terrier called Whisky who would have sat thus draped forever. I came to the conclusion that he either thought it pleased his slightly odd owner, or he was waiting patiently for my next move in some new game that he imagined I had invented. When eventually I removed the towel, Whisky would simply cock his head and look at me rather curiously!

2. Packet puzzler

This simple test is quick and easy to arrange. It is suitable for any breed, although short-nosed dogs like pekes and pugs tend to be slower at it than those with longer snouts. However, time taken is not involved in the scoring, which looks only at the method employed by the dog to solve the problem. Do not cheat by waiting until your dog is really hungry before setting this test.

You will need:
- Square of stiff paper
- Favorite food treat

What to do
1. Place the food treat in the square of paper and fold it twice to enclose the food.
2. Now put the packet down in front of your dog and watch how he sets about getting the treat.

What's his score?

3 points if your dog uses only his paws to open the packet.

2 points if he uses his mouth and paws to open the packet.

1 point if he doesn't try to open the packet but proceeds to play with it.

1 bonus point if your dog is a short-nosed type but shows real determination in trying to open the packet.

3. Peekaboo 1

In this test your dog has to think about what's going on and then take appropriate action in order to get the food treat. Pastoral breeds tend to excel here.

You will need:

- Large piece of cardboard (for dimensions, see step 1)
- Some blocks or boxes, suitable for supporting the barrier
- Favorite food treat

What to do

1. Construct a cardboard barrier 5 feet wide and higher than the dog when he stands on his hind legs. Cut a 3-inch-wide vertical slot in the center running from 4 inches from the top to 4 inches from the bottom. Support the barrier with the blocks or boxes.

2. Stand on one side of the barrier with your dog on the other and show him a food treat at the slot. Watch what he does.

What's his score?

5 points if your dog comes around the barrier in under 30 seconds.

3 points if he comes around the barrier in around 30–60 seconds.

0 points if he pushes his head into the slot and gets stuck, or keeps pushing, or doesn't try at all.

4. Peekaboo 2

This test challenges your pet's problem-solving skills. A bright dog achieves his aim of coming to you by first running away.

You will need:
- Suitable fence or wall (see step 1)

What to do

1. Arrange for your dog to be on the other side of a fence or cardboard barrier from you, with a gap through which he can see you but cannot pass.
2. Call your dog and see what he does.

What's his score?

5 points if your dog comes to you by running around one end of the barrier, or jumping over the barrier, or trying to jump over, failing, and then running around the end of the barrier.

2 points if he tries to jump over the barrier, fails, and then just sits there.

0 points if he doesn't try to get to you, but just sits there and perhaps whines.

5. Mega maze

Seeing how long your dog takes to find his way out of a maze is a superb test of problem-solving intelligence and a favorite with behavioral scientists. Why not invite your friends and their dogs to a summer maze competition and party?

You will need:

- Large outdoor area
- Plenty of wooden boards or boxes
- Stopwatch, or wristwatch, with a second hand

What to do

1. One suitable design for a maze is shown here. It does not need to be very complicated, but should include at least five or six dead ends. The walls should be high enough to discourage your pet from simply jumping over them.

2. When you have built your maze, put your dog in the center and leave immediately. Do not call him or make any other sound until he emerges. Time how long it takes him to find his way out.

What's his score?

10 points if your dog takes up to 3 minutes to emerge from the maze illustrated right.

5 points if he takes 3–6 minutes.

3 points if he takes 6–9 minutes.

1 point if he takes more than 9 minutes but eventually makes it.

0 points if he doesn't get out, and perhaps cries plaintively for help.

Scientists found that, at first, shelties and fox terriers performed poorly while beagles and basenjis excelled. The beagles' aptitude was due to their quick exploratory movements, a trait of a breed developed to hunt small game, while the basenjis' keen vision enabled them to pick up clues leading to a solution. With repetition, the shelties and terriers improved markedly due to their skill at learning repetitive behaviors, while the beagles' inquisitive nature, which produces variable behavior, led to a deterioration.

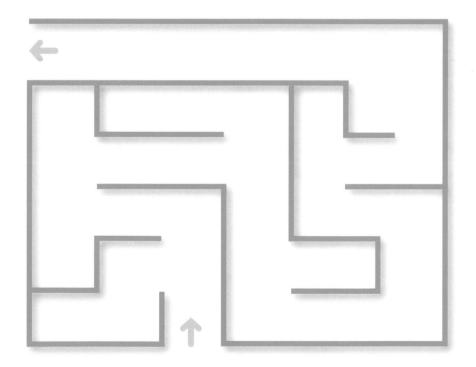

6. Mini maze

This mini maze test is very easy to construct and ideal for use indoors if you do not have access to an outdoor area suitable for the larger maze on pages 58–59. You will need to teach your dog the "sit-stay" command first (see pages 164–165).

You will need:

- Pieces of cardboard
- Adhesive tape
- Food treat or a favorite toy
- Stopwatch, or wristwatch, with a second hand

What to do

1. Using adhesive tape, stick together as many pieces of cardboard as necessary to form a long rectangle.
2. Stand the cardboard on its long side and bend it into a U shape. The sides of the U should be slightly taller than your dog when he stands on his hind legs, and each side at least twice the length of his body.
3. Cut a hole 1½ inches in diameter in the U shape at its center point, at a height that will allow your dog to see through it when he is standing on all four legs.
4. Put your dog on the inside of the U shape and give the "sit-stay" command (see pages 164–165).
5. Move to the outside of the U shape and hold a treat close to the hole. Watch what he does.

What's his score?

10 points if your dog immediately turns, comes out of the U and around to you to collect the treat.

6 points if he comes out and around to collect the treat within 1 minute.

2 points if he comes out and around to collect the treat in 1–3 minutes.

0 points if he pushes down the cardboard to get at the treat.

7. Tracking

This is fun to do when out for a walk with a friend and your dog. It isn't a test of intelligence so much as an indicator of your pet's sense of smell. Unsuitable for short-nosed breeds, this test works best with scent hounds, the larger spaniels, and most pastoral breeds.

You will need:

- Helper
- Access to an area with suitable hiding places
- Time for a long walk

What to do

1. Pick a suitable path for your walk, then after a little while put the lead on your dog and give it to your helper to hold. Walk ahead by 110–215 yards and, out of sight of your dog, find a hiding place at least 12 feet off to one side of the path. Call to your helper but then remain silent.

2. Your helper should now release your dog. He will (hopefully) begin tracking you by picking up your scent. Your helper now continues walking along the path behind your dog; when they are level with your hiding place, they should not acknowledge you but keep walking straight ahead. Your dog may either track you down by leaving the path or prefer to accompany your helper along it.

What's his score?

5 points if your dog comes straight to you.

2 points if he tracks you up to the point where you left the path, but then waits for and accompanies your friend.

0 points if he doesn't bother to track you at all.

8. Find the food

This is a very simple test, but one that assesses your dog's problem-solving powers and ability to take appropriate action to resolve it. Short-nosed breeds will find this test more difficult than those with longer snouts, and I have found mutts particularly adept.

You will need:
- Generous chunk of your dog's favorite food
- Low table
- Stopwatch, or wristwatch, with a second hand

What to do
1. Make sure your dog is watching you with his full attention. Show him the food treat and let him sniff it.
2. With your dog watching, slowly place the food under the table where he could reach it with an outstretched paw.
3. Start timing, while verbally urging your dog to retrieve the food.

What's his score?

5 points if your dog retrieves the food using his paws alone, in less than 1 minute.

4 points if he retrieves the food using his paws alone, in 1–3 minutes, or using only his snout, in up to 3 minutes.

3 points if he uses his snout alone but has not retrieved the food after 3 minutes.

2 points if he sniffs and tries a couple of times with his snout but does not retrieve the food.

0 points if he makes no attempt to retrieve the food after 3 minutes.

Top tips

Naturally, the hungrier your dog is at the time you try this test the better he will perform. The food you select is also a factor—make sure it really is his favorite!

9. Canny canine

Another simple test that examines the problem-solving skill of your dog, this is ideal entertainment for a rainy day when you both have to be indoors. As a benchmark, I tried this test on a Labrador and a pug—both scored 4 points.

You will need:

- Helper (optional)
- Empty food can
- Favorite food treat
- Stopwatch, or wristwatch, with a second hand

What to do

1. Command your dog to "sit-stay" (see pages 164–165), or have a helper hold on to him.
2. Show him the tasty food treat and let him sniff it thoroughly.
3. With your dog's full attention, slowly place the treat on the floor about 6 feet away from him and invert the can over the treat.
4. Start timing and verbally encourage your dog to get the treat.

What's his score?

5 points if your dog knocks over the can and grabs the treat in 5 seconds or less.

4 points if he knocks over the can and grabs the treat in 5 15 seconds.

3 points if he knocks over the can and grabs the treat in 15–30 seconds.

2 points if he knocks over the can and grabs the treat in 30–60 seconds.

1 point if he knocks over the can and grabs the treat in 1–3 minutes.

0 points if he inspects the can and sniffs at it, but doesn't proceed to knock it over.

1 bonus point if he uses a paw rather than his nose to knock over the can.

10. Treat under towel

This is another food retrieval test, designed to examine how your pet carries out appropriate action to solve a problem. Some dogs, especially short-nosed breeds, find it a little more difficult than the Canny Canine test on pages 66–67. Terrier-type dogs, bred originally to work underground, are particularly good at it.

You will need:

- Helper (optional)
- Generous chunk of your dog's favorite food
- Hand towel
- Stopwatch, or wristwatch, with a second hand

What to do

1. Command your dog to "sit-stay" (see pages 164–165) or have a helper hold on to him.
2. Show your dog the treat and let him sniff it.
3. Slowly place the treat about 6 feet away from him. With your dog watching you, cover the treat with the towel.
4. Start timing and verbally encourage your dog to get the treat.

What's his score?

Most dogs get at the food by thrusting their noses under the towel:

5 points if your dog retrieves the treat in less than 15 seconds.

4 points if he retrieves the treat in 15–30 seconds.

3 points if he retrieves the treat in 30–60 seconds.

2 points if he tries to retrieve the treat but gives up.

0 points if he makes no attempt to retrieve the treat.

1 bonus point if he retrieves the treat by biting the towel and lifting it away from the food.

11. Treat and fence

Assuming your dog enjoys food treats, this test is one of the easiest. It requires him to employ a combination of his powers of observation, memory, and problem solving. Alert, lively individuals tend to fare better at it than more sleepy, preoccupied ones.

You will need:
- Smelly favorite food treat
- Access to a suitable garden or yard with a fence or wall

Caution
Do not carry out this test if there is a busy road on the other side of the fence or wall.

What to do
1. Take your dog out into the garden or back yard on the lead. Walk him along the fence or wall and past the gate, which must be left open. Show him the food treat and let him smell it.
2. Toss the treat over the fence or wall. Let go of the lead and watch what your dog does next.

What's his score?
3 points if your dog at once dashes back to the gate and disappears through it in search of the food treat—it doesn't matter if he cannot find it or decides not to eat it.

0 points if he carries on walking with you or just sniffs around.

Location, location, location
If you do not have a suitable fence or wall on your property, wait until you are out in a park or the countryside and find a suitable location there. Should this prove absolutely impossible, give your pet 3 points anyway so that his grand total score is not affected.

How did he do?

Domestic dogs have inherited the various skills of their wild relatives but, as we have seen, because of artificial selection by man the breeds display their abilities in different ways. In addition, dogs often have their own opinions and clearly think for themselves.

Human by design

If dogs perform indifferently in tests designed by humans, it doesn't necessarily mean they are stupid. The tests are artificial and may not tap into their ancient talents. Your dog may not understand why you are putting the treat under a towel or a can when you normally give it to him directly, and will maybe wait for you to return to your senses! This is one reason why the tests should be treated as games: dogs love to play.

Lateral thinking

Thinking for themselves may mean some dogs prefer to do things their way, which may not be the same as their owners' way.

Some police dogs fail their entrance exams because they are *too* intelligent. They are trained to attack people by biting them on the arm, which involves practicing on someone wearing a padded suit with especially thick protection on the arms. Some bright dogs don't make the grade because instead of

going for the arms they aim at the throat or stomach, and so are considered too dangerous for police work. In fact, the dog has worked out during training that an arm bite doesn't hurt and so reasons he should go for a more effective—and damaging—hold.

Problem-solving score

It's now time to add up your dog's score for this section:

60 points or more Very intelligent.
55–59 points Above average.
50–54 points Average.
Less than 50 points Needs improvement, through regular repetition and training (see pages 152–177).

Section B
Analytical powers tests

The ability to analyze a situation was vital to our dogs' wild ancestors. As a pack animal, a dog needed to be able to calculate how many of his fellow pack members, enemies, or quarry were nearby when out hunting. This analytical skill has been passed down to domestic dogs: there are many stories of sheepdogs searching for a missing member of the flock.

Canine calculation

Even more remarkable is the evidence that dogs can automatically carry out advanced mathematical calculations. Dr. Penning, an American mathematician, noticed that when he took his corgi, Elvis, to the beach and threw a ball out into the waves for the dog to retrieve, the animal always took the optimal path, on land and then in the water, to minimize total travel time.

Armed with a stopwatch and measuring tape, Dr. Penning carried out repeated ball-retrieving experiments with Elvis. No matter which path the dog chose and whatever his running and swimming speeds, the time he took was always the minimum and closely matched a calculus-based model of the situation. Dogs apparently make an instantaneous "global" mental decision at the outset as to which is the best path to take.

The tests

The tests that follow are among the most fascinating since they involve your dog's inbuilt, involuntary skills. They demonstrate how even the most pampered pet of the fanciest breed still retains the ability of his wild, pack-hunting ancestors to compute aspects of the world around him.

Analytical powers tests 75

12. Canine accountancy

This test was originally applied successfully to human babies and it works just as well with dogs, particularly mutts. It proves that your pet can do simple addition and subtraction by using his powers of observation and reasoning, and actually counting.

You will need:

- 10–12 identical objects, such as colored balls
- Board to be used as a screen
- Brick or other weight
- Stopwatch, or wristwatch, with a second hand

What to do

1. Sit on the floor with your dog about 6 feet away from you. Place the screen between you, supported by a brick or other weight. Show the dog one ball above the screen, then lower it behind your side of the screen and place it on the floor. Continue until you have shown six or seven balls to your dog.

2. Remove the screen so that your dog can see the group of balls. Look at your dog's eyes: Is he staring at the balls? If so, time the duration of his gaze. This is his basic "gaze time."

3. Replace the screen and then remove or add a ball or balls, or leave the number unchanged, unseen by your pet.

4. Remove the screen so that your dog can again see the group of balls. Again, time the duration of his gaze.

5. Repeat the procedure ten times, each time changing or retaining the number of balls and measuring the time for which your dog stares at them. A longer gaze time indicates that your dog has spotted something amiss and detected your duplicity.

What's his score?

2 points if his gaze time is longer when more than four balls in total are involved.

1 point if your dog's gaze time is longer when you add or remove a ball or balls.

13. Canine calculator

This is not so much a test like all the others, but rather a chance to reflect on what has been discovered about dogs' remarkable mental powers. When you are out on a walk with your dog on a beach or by an inland stretch of water, do what Dr. Penning did but without the need for a stopwatch and measuring tape.

You will need:
- Access to a large area of water
- Time for a walk
- Favorite ball or toy

What to do

1. Throw a ball or toy out onto the water and get your dog to fetch it.
2. Your pet will then calculate the ideal route that will take the minimum time. He may plunge in where you are and paddle straight to the ball, he may run along the water's edge until directly opposite the toy and then go in, or he may run part of the way on land and then swim off at an angle. I am not asking you to make mathematical computations, but you can be sure that, following the discovery of Dr. Penning, confirmed by other scientists, your dog will take the fastest, most efficient route.
3. Try it several times. How he does it may change, but each time the route will be the quickest way to reach the ball or toy.

What's his score?

2 points if your dog brings back the ball or toy at the first time of asking.

0 points if your dog fails to bring back the ball or toy at the first time of asking.

How did he do?

These tests have given us a glimpse of the surprisingly sophisticated mental powers of the dog. Without looking into the theories of those who believe dogs possess extrasensory perception, we know enough about the intelligence of these amazing animals to realize that, whether show-dog pedigree or mixed-up mutt, your dog is very, very special.

Circus act

You have probably seen numerous dogs performing unbelievable feats of counting in variety shows or circuses. However, in almost all cases, trickery is involved. The animals bark, then tap a foot or ring a bell when a certain number has been reached—but this is in response to some inconspicuous signal from their handler that the audience cannot detect. Of course, these dogs have been remarkably well trained, but they are not actually counting. Nevertheless they, like all dogs, possess an innate counting ability (see pages 76–77).

Analytical powers score

It's now time to add up your dog's score for this section, which includes the ten "challenges" of Canine Accountancy (pages 76–77) plus the 2 points given for retrieval of the ball in the Canine Calculator (pages 78–79) test:

15 points or more Very intelligent.

12–14 points Above average.

8–11 points Average.

Less than 8 points Needs improvement, through regular repetition and training (see pages 152–177).

Section C
General IQ tests

This section presents a number of simple tests for intelligent behavior. They cover aspects of canine mental ability such as analytical, observational, and problem-solving power. Mutts tend to excel at them as their inherited melting pot of genes from forebears of all kinds endows them with "hybrid vigor" that is mental as well as physical.

Are we testing IQ?

Some tests that have been devised for dogs have attracted criticism as not being reliable indicators of canine intelligence. This is mainly because the scoring depends on the subjective interpretations of the human observers.

Where obedience is involved, some experts question whether this is really a good measure of intelligence. Terriers, for example, don't generally do very well in tests where obedience plays a part, but their slowness in responding to new commands does not mean they are unintelligent—rather that they are independent souls who are not overly concerned about doting on their owners!

Repetition

A dog's performance in these tests will also be affected by the number of times it is repeated. As we saw on pages 58–59, some breeds such as terriers and shelties are likely to improve their score with repetition. Beagles, on the other hand, generally do not. Overall, the breeds that tend to score highest in general IQ tests are the German shepherd, border collie and poodle.

14. Outdoor treasure hunt 1

This test involves your dog's general intelligence and tracking powers. Spaniels, scent hounds and German Shepherds generally do well at it, while toy breeds score better in indoor treasure hunts (see pages 108–111). This test is best carried out when there are no other dogs in the vicinity.

You will need:

- Access to an area with suitable hiding places
- Time for a walk
- Pocketful of your dog's favorite food treats
- Stopwatch, or wristwatch, with a second hand

What to do

1. Take your dog for a walk in a park or large garden. As you go, in full view of your dog hide a treat—for example, behind a tree trunk, in a clump of grass, on a fence, or on a low branch of a bush. Do not allow him to start searching until you give permission, then start timing.
2. Repeat the process ten times during your walk. Hopefully, your dog will find the treat and either gobble it down or bring it back to you on each occasion.

What's his score?

The total possible score for finding all ten treats is 20:

2 points if your dog finds the treat in less than 3 minutes.

1 point if he finds the treat in 3 minutes or over.

0 points if you have to give any sort of clue or assistance to set your pet on the right track.

15. Outdoor treasure hunt 2

This is similar to the previous test (see pages 84–85) but requires your dog to have been trained to "sit-stay" (see pages 164–165). Again, it tests your dog's general intelligence and tracking powers.

You will need:

- Access to a large outdoor area
- Favorite toy
- Stopwatch, or wristwatch, with a second hand

What to do

1. Take your dog for a walk in a park or open countryside. Command him to "sit-stay" and then walk away. When you are at least 165 yards away from him, drop the toy onto one of your footprints.

2. Walk back to your dog by a different route and then send him off to search for his toy. The aim is for him to follow the scent of your shoes, hopefully come across his toy, and retrieve it.

3. Repeat the test five times in all.

What's his score?

The total possible score for five retrieves is 10 points:

2 points if your dog retrieves the toy in less than 2 minutes.

1 point if he retrieves the toy in 2 minutes or more, but without any clues or assistance from you.

0 points if you have to give any clues or assistance in the retrieval.

Light and weather

You will find that, understandably, weather conditions may affect your dog's performance in the Outdoor Treasure Hunts. Where scent plays a part, humid air after rain will enhance his sniffing abilities. Bright sunlight assists your pet's visual powers, but with his eyes better able to see in the dark than yours, it is fascinating to see how well he can perform after the sun goes down. Try it, but take a flashlight just in case.

16. Advanced treasure hunt 1

This test can be performed either indoors or out. It is essentially an enjoyable game that will enhance your dog's hunting and tracking abilities, and can be accomplished by all breeds.

You will need:

Object to be retrieved:

- For hunting and tracking breeds that usually retrieve quickly—a favorite toy
- For dogs with better vision but less scenting skill, such as sight hounds, and pets that do not have a favorite toy—a stronger-smelling food treat such as a cube of hard cheese

What to do

1. Throw the object a short distance away and tell your dog to "fetch."
2. Repeat a number of times, gradually increasing the distance up to about 55 yards.

What's his score?

5 points when your dog retrieves the object correctly on ten consecutive throws at varying distances over $5\frac{1}{2}$ yards.

4 points for eight or nine correct retrieves.

3 points for six or seven correct retrieves.

2 points for four or five correct retrieves.

1 point for two or three correct retrieves.

17. Advanced treasure hunt 2

For this test your dog should already be trained to "sit-stay" (see pages 164–165). Once again, this test can be performed indoors or out. It is particularly suitable for the garden.

You will need:

Object to be retrieved:

• For hunting and tracking breeds that usually retrieve quickly—a favorite toy

• For dogs with better vision but less scenting skill, such as sight hounds, and pets that do not have a favorite toy—a stronger-smelling food treat such as a cube of hard cheese

What to do

1. Give the "sit-stay" command and then, in full view of your dog, hide the object where it can be found easily. Go back to your pet and command, "Find it."

2. When your dog returns with his "find," praise him and offer a treat. Repeat a number of times, eventually phasing out the food reward.

What's his score?

5 points when your dog returns with his "find" ten times.

4 points for eight or nine correct retrieves.

3 points for six or seven correct retrieves.

2 points for four or five correct retrieves.

1 point for two or three correct retrieves.

18. Advanced treasure hunt 3

This test is a more difficult variation of the previous two (see pages 88–89). Toy breeds such as the King Charles spaniel and Yorkshire terrier tend to be particularly good performers.

You will need:

Object to be retrieved:

- For hunting and tracking breeds that usually retrieve quickly—a favorite toy
- For dogs with better vision but less scenting skill, such as sight hounds, and pets that do not have a favorite toy—a stronger-smelling food treat such as a cube of hard cheese

What to do

1. Give the "sit-stay" command and then, in full view of your dog, hide the object where it can be found with a little difficulty—perhaps partly behind a chair or other piece of furniture, or a tree if you are outdoors.
2. Go back to your pet and command, "Find it."
3. When your dog returns with his "find," praise him and, in the early stages, give a food treat.
4. Repeat a number of times, gradually phasing out the food reward and increasing the difficulty of the test, until you are hiding the object completely out of your dog's sight.

What's his score?

5 points when your dog retrieves the object correctly ten times.

4 points for eight or nine correct retrieves.

3 points for six or seven correct retrieves.

2 points for four or five correct retrieves.

1 point for two or three correct retrieves.

19. Advanced treasure hunt 4

When your dog has done well in the previous three tests, you can both proceed to this one—the most difficult. Here, your dog does not see you hide the object: he truly has to hunt.

You will need:

Object to be retrieved:
- For hunting and tracking breeds that usually retrieve quickly—a favorite toy
- For dogs with better vision but less scenting skill, such as sight hounds, and pets that do not have a favorite toy—a stronger-smelling food treat such as a cube of hard cheese

What to do

1. Put the dog indoors or outside as appropriate so that you are out of his sight, and then hide the object as in the previous test.
2. Once it is hidden, let your dog join you again and say, "Find it." Repeat several times, beginning with the object partially visible and progressing until it is completely hidden.

What's his score?

5 points when your dog finds the object on ten consecutive challenges.

4 points for eight or nine correct retrieves.

3 points for six or seven correct retrieves.

2 points for four or five correct retrieves.

1 point for two or three correct retrieves.

20. Obstacle course

In this test your dog will tackle a series of obstacles in much the same way that soldiers undergo assault course training! As well as being great fun for both of you, this will instill confidence and promote agility in your pet. It is suitable for any breed except very short-legged types like dachshunds or, of course, individuals with arthritis or other forms of handicap.

You will need:
- Large outdoor space
- Hurdles
- Tire
- Tunnel
- Ramp
- Long lead (optional)
- Favorite food treats or toy

What to do

Build the obstacles in your course using materials that cannot injure your dog: no jagged edges or protrusions, and no toxic paint. Structures should be stable, but with the bars on hurdles loose so that they will fall off easily if clipped by the dog's foot.

Hurdle

Your hurdle should be no higher than the height to which your dog has jumped during training (see page 95).

Tire

Hang a large car tire from a children's swingset frame or something similar. Suspend it using several ropes or chains hung from different directions, so that the tire barely moves.

Tunnel

Cover half-hoops or angled sticks with paper, sheets, or wooden board to make a tunnel large enough for your

Small is beautiful

If you cannot buy—or do not want to make—the obstacles as suggested, a scaled-down course constructed from boxes, canes, and cardboard is still appropriate. Improvise to see what works, but ensure safety and try to test your dog's jumping, balance, and general agility.

dog to pass through easily. Begin with a tunnel about 3 feet long, then increase the length and introduce bends over time.

Ramp

This is basically a slatted wooden plane that is angled to whatever height you require—usually about 2 feet high at first.

When you first introduce your dog to the course, use all the familiar commands as appropriate. Encourage him to pass through or over each obstacle by luring him with food treats or a toy, plus enthusiastic verbal and body language. Accompany him all the way through and reward with plenty of praise and treats when he has completed the course. If necessary at first, use a long lead to help guide him.

As your dog becomes more experienced, make the tunnel longer and more complex, raise the ramp angle, and add a second tyre and hurdle.

What's his score?

10 points when for the first time your dog clears the course smoothly, quickly, and without any hesitation, or without damaging or dislodging any of the obstacles.

2 points for each obstacle he has negotiated well if he does not complete the entire course correctly.

Training your dog to jump

1. Construct a low hurdle that your dog can easily walk over. Put him on a long lead and walk him at heel over the hurdle several times in both directions.

2. Place your dog on one side of the hurdle in the "sit-stay" position (see pages 164–165) and walk to the other side. Call him to come to you. As he approaches the hurdle, give the command "jump" and begin to walk backwards while reeling in the lead.

3. When your dog has jumped the hurdle, have him sit facing you and give plenty of praise. Continue in this way over several sessions until he does not need the lead to guide him.

4. When your dog jumps reliably on command, begin increasing the height of the hurdle in 1- or 2-inch increments, to a maximum of one-and-a-half times the dog's own height.

21. Hide-and-seek

You and your pet may well consider this simply a good game, just like the one you used to play as a child, and so it is—but it also involves the dog employing all of his senses and can be used as a test of the animal's basic intelligence. It is suitable for all breeds, but especially toy and terrier types since it requires neither physical strength nor specially acute senses, just inquisitiveness and a sense of fun. Hide-and-seek is for indoors, not outside in the street or a busy park.

You will need:

- Favorite food treats

What to do

1. Give your dog the "sit-stay" command (see pages 164–165) and then go off to find a suitable hiding place. Once you are hidden, call your dog by name and then remain still and silent. If you can tell he is moving in the wrong direction you can call him again, but do not do this continuously or he will simply home in on your voice.

2. When your dog discovers you, give him a food treat and lots of well-deserved praise.

3. Repeat the process six times, and then score him according to how he performs on the sixth occasion.

What's his score?

5 points if your dog finds you within 1 minute.

3 points if he finds you in 1–2 minutes.

2 points if he finds you in 2–3 minutes.

0 points if he takes longer than 3 minutes to find you.

22. New words

This test was devised by the eminent professor of psychology at the University of British Columbia, Stanley Coren. It aims to examine your dog's core intelligence by addressing him using a word that is new to him, whereupon he realizes, crucially, that you are talking to him.

You will need:
- Imagination
- Your dog's attention

What to do

1. Get your pet to settle down about 6 feet in front of you.

2. Using the tone of voice in which you normally address him, call "Refrigerator!" (The choice of word is not important.) Your dog is not expected to think that, all of a sudden, he has been transformed into an icebox, but simply to realize that you are addressing him. It is important that you look steadily at the dog while doing this. He has to know that you are communicating both verbally and visually. He hears a multitude of words uttered by you in the house each day that are clearly not directed at him. You are not trying to give your pet a new name but rather getting him to realize that he is being addressed. Change the word used every time you repeat the test.

What's his score?

7 points if your dog shows a response of any kind.

If he does not come to you, call "Television" (or "Pigsty" or "Influenza" or whatever you like) in the same tone of voice.

6 points if he comes to you.

If your dog has still not responded, call his name.

5 points if he comes to you or shows any tendency to move towards you.

If your dog has still not moved, call his name a second time.

4 points if he comes to you.

1 point if he still does not come to you.

23. Smiley face

Doing this test will make you smile! It involves a key characteristic of man's best friend, one that has been arguably the most important in the process of domestication: the ability to interact with, understand, and "read" the human being. Studying your face and interpreting its expressions is more important to your pet than understanding the other aspects of your body language, and all breeds are capable of performing this test equally well.

You will need:

• Your ability to grin

What to do

1. Have your dog lying or sitting about 6 feet away from you. You must not have told him to sit or stay: simply pick a time when he happens to be comfortably in this position.
2. Now stare intently at your dog's face. When he looks directly at you, count to three silently and then smile broadly. Watch for his reaction.

What's his score?

5 points if your dog comes to you promptly with his tail wagging.

4 points if he comes slowly or only part of the way, or with no tail wag.

3 points if he stands or rises to a sit, but doesn't move toward you.

2 points if he moves away from you.

0 points if he pays no attention.

Can dogs smile?

Although some dogs do naturally adopt facial expressions that resemble smiles—Samoyeds and dalmatians are said to be the "smiliest" breeds—they are not the equivalent of human smiles of pleasure or amusement. Any dog can be trained to "smile" on command, but this is really just a party trick.

24. Cup and treat

This variation on the Canny Canine test (see pages 66–67) explores your pet's general level of intelligence. Memory and basic reasoning power are involved.

You will need:
- Helper
- Two cups
- Favorite food treats
- Stopwatch, or wristwatch, with a second hand

What to do

1. While your helper holds your pet, invert the cups and place a treat under one of them. Make sure your dog watches you do this.
2. Take your dog out of the room for 15 minutes. In his absence, place a treat under the other cup as well. This prevents the dog using his sense of smell to find the correct treat.
3. Bring him back in and see if he goes straight for the cup under which you put the first treat.

What's his score?

4 points if your dog goes straight to the correct cup, knocks it over, and takes the treat.

3 points if he goes straight to the correct cup, but takes more than 15 seconds before he knocks it over.

2 points if he goes to the correct cup but does not knock it over in under 1 minute.

0 points if he goes to the wrong cup and knocks it over or does not pay much attention to either cup.

25. New toy

This test is very simple and relies to a large extent on your pet's natural curiosity. Dogs with a keen zest for life usually perform best at this test.

You will need:
- Exciting new toy
- Towel

What to do
1. Show your dog the toy and allow him to inspect it closely.
2. Place the toy on the floor and slowly cover it with the towel. Watch your dog's reaction.

What's his score?
4 points if your dog goes to the towel and tries (successfully or not) to retrieve the toy.

0 points if he makes no attempt.

How did he do?

The tests in this section may have been simple, but they have all probed your pet's IQ in ways that animal psychologists consider very valuable. No other animal species could perform so well in these tests or, in most cases, even do them at all.

Compatible creatures

With its combination of highly tuned senses, powers of memory, reasoning, analysis and problem solving, and the ability to interact so closely with human beings, canine intelligence is the engine that drove successful domestication. It is also the reason why your dog is such a beloved and important member of your household.

Greater than the sum of its parts

Intelligence tests like those in this section are good for investigating individual aspects of a dog's mental abilities, but no single test or group of tests can be used to judge the animal's intelligence as a whole. When we consider wonderfully intelligent dogs such as Rigel and Dorado (see pages 34–37), it is the totality of their achievement that we admire. Both dogs brought a whole kaleidoscope of talents into play.

General IQ score

It's now time to add up your dog's score for this section:

75 points or more Very intelligent.
60–74 points Above average.
45–59 points Average.
Less than 45 points Needs improvement, through regular repetition and
  training (see pages 152–177).

Section D
Memory and observation tests

Memory is a key component of intelligence and dogs possess five main areas in their brains, listed below. Nevertheless, it seems unlikely that they can recall an item stored in their memory at will, but rather that it must be evoked by some sort of associated stimulus, such as a particular smell or sound.

Canine memory types

Event memory Remembering events that have occurred.

Semantic memory Remembering facts.

Motor memory Remembering movement (for example, how to catch something).

Spatial memory Remembering places and carrying mental maps of home territory.

Social memory Remembering which person or other animal has been friendly and which has not.

Memory loss?

Some dog psychologists believe that when an owner goes on vacation, boarding their pet in kennels, the animal loses all memory of them—just as if they had never existed. Only when the owner returns from holiday is the dog's memory triggered by familiar sounds, smells, and sights, and consequently the person "comes into existence" once more. To put it another way: dogs do not think about their owners when separated from them. Other experts consider that when a dog has been separated from his owner for over ten hours the animal's feelings of rejection fade away, along with the image of the owner in his mind.

The tests

It's now time to run your pet through some intelligence tests that depend on his memory and challenge both short- and long-term aspects.

Memory and observation tests 107

26. Indoor treasure hunt 1

This is an easy test that is very entertaining for both you and your dog. It is ideal for small and medium-sized breeds, and depends more on the animal's short-term memory than his overall intelligence. Nevertheless, "brighter" individuals usually perform better. As with other tests, regular repetition will ensure your pet improves his score rapidly.

You will need:
- Favorite food treats
- Stopwatch, or wristwatch, with a second hand

What to do

1. Accompanied by your dog, walk around your home hiding six edible treats in a variety of places, all within reach yet not easy to see—for example, beneath a bed, under a cushion, behind a sofa, and so on. It is important to let your dog see what you are doing. When hiding the treats, be sure to walk all around each room, not simply straight to the hiding place. This prevents your dog finding the treats by merely tracking your footsteps. Hide ten treats in total. It may be best to make a note of their locations for use when scoring.

2. Now take your dog into a room where nothing has been hidden. Wait for 30 seconds and then release him to search the house while you begin timing. Follow him in silence and see how many treats he can find.

What's his score?

Total possible score for ten quick finds is 30:

3 points for each treat your dog finds in under 3 minutes.

2 points for each treat he finds in 3–6 minutes.

1 point for each treat he finds in 6–12 minutes.

27. Indoor treasure hunt 2

Indoor Treasure Hunt 1 (see pages 108–109) challenged your dog's short-term memory. Now you can engage his long-term memory by carrying out the same test but with one important modification—extra time.

You will need:
- Favorite food treats
- Stopwatch, or wristwatch, with a second hand

What to do

1. Accompanied by your dog, walk around your home hiding ten edible treats in a variety of places, all within reach yet not easy to see—for example, beneath a bed, under a cushion, behind a sofa, and so on. It is important to let your dog see what you are doing. When hiding the treats, be sure to walk all around each room, not simply straight to the hiding place. This prevents your dog finding the treats by merely tracking your footsteps.

2. Now take your dog into a room where nothing has been hidden. Wait for 10 minutes and then release him to search the house while you time. Follow him in silence and see how many treats he can find.

What's his score?

Total possible score for ten quick finds is 30:

3 points for each treat your dog finds in under 3 minutes.

2 points for each treat he finds in 3–6 minutes.

1 point for each treat he finds in 6–12 minutes.

Rico's tests

All dogs have a well-developed memory bank in which they store words spoken by humans. Rico was a Border Collie living in Germany who could recognize the names of over 200 of his toys—call out the name of a particular toy and he would fetch the correct item 93 percent of the time! Rico's three tests assess your dog's ability to accumulate a vocabulary.

28. Test 1

You will need:
- A number of different objects such as plastic toys
- Favorite food treats

What to do

1. Throw one object for your dog and say "Fetch the . . ."
2. When he retrieves it and brings it back to you, give plenty of praise and a treat. Repeat again with the same object until your dog is quick and reliable in response.

29. Test 2

What to do

1. Throw a different object for you dog and say "Fetch the . . ."
2. When he retrieves it and brings it back to you, give praise and a treat. Repeat the process until once again your dog is retrieving the object quickly and reliably.

30. Test 3
What to do
1. Throw both toys together and ask your dog to fetch a specific one. When he retrieves the correct one and brings it back to you, give plenty of praise and a treat.
2. Increase the number of objects and continue in the same manner.

What's his score?
20 points if your dog has learned thirty words.
15 points if he has learned fifteen words.
10 points if he has learned ten words.
5 points if he has learned five words.

Find the treat

This test is a useful measure of canine intelligence and depends on your pet having a good memory. It is suitable for any breed: Afghan hounds, Pekingese, border collies, and mutts have all achieved equally high scores. It isn't the breed that counts in a test like this, but the IQ of the individual animal.

31. Test 1

You will need:

- Five or six identical containers, such as cans or non-transparent storage jars, with tight-fitting, screw-on lids
- Favorite food treats

What to do

1. Show a treat to your dog and then, in full view, open one container and put the treat inside it. Replace the lid firmly.

2. Shuffle all the containers around on the floor, keeping your eye on the one containing the treat.

3. Your dog now has to find the correct container, helped only by a signal from you, and to be successful this must be his first choice. Say nothing when starting the test, but simply point at the correct tin or jar—this is the only signal your dog receives. If he gets it right and goes to the correct container, open it and give him the treat and lots of praise. If he gets it wrong, repeat the whole procedure from the beginning.

32. Test 2

What to do

Once your dog has mastered your pointing signal in Test 1, move on to indicating in some other way such as nodding or even just staring fixedly at the correct container.

What's his score?

The highest total for both tests together is 24 points:

12 points if your dog learns each signal in fewer than four repetitions.
8 points if he learns each signal after 4–10 repetitions.
6 points if he takes more than ten repetitions, but eventually gets there.

33. Spot the difference 1

This memory and observation test depends on your pet being familiar with the time of day you take him out for a walk and the preparations that precede it, such as putting on your coat and picking up his lead.

You will need:
- Your coat
- Your dog's lead

What to do

1. At a time of day when you do not usually go for a walk, put on your coat but do not call your dog or go to the door.
2. Wait to see how your dog reacts to your actions.

What's his score?

10 points if your dog brings his lead to you or, if he cannot reach it, at least goes and sits by it.

8 points if he immediately dashes either to the door or to you.

0 points if he does not react at all.

34. Spot the difference 2

This simple test again challenges your dog's powers of observation and memory. It is very easy to set up—no special equipment required!

You will need:
• Some time and imagination!

What to do

1. When your dog is outside, rearrange some of the furniture in a room with which he is familiar. Perhaps add a chair or a big sofa cushion, change the position of the television set, and so on.
2. When your dog returns to the room, watch how he reacts to the changed surroundings.

What's his score?

10 points if your dog immediately spots that things have changed and starts exploring and sniffing.

0 points if he doesn't. Your pet is clearly one of those who has no interest whatsoever in interior design!

How did he do?

Linking observation and memory in the tests in this section enabled your dog to demonstrate his intelligence in some entertaining ways. Rather surprisingly, scientists at the University of Michigan reckon that a dog's short-term memory lasts a mere 5 minutes, as compared to 16 hours for the domestic cat. Most dog owners, including myself, would probably beg to disagree!

More memory types

Analyzing the span of a dog's long-term memory is even more complicated. In addition to the five different forms of canine memory described on pages 106–107, we can divide long-term memory into two forms: real and associative.

Real memory is the long-term storage of observed and other sensory images and experiences in the brain. This type of memory probably lies behind the behavior of a dog that grieves for a lost owner and over the long term utterly rejects the idea of settling into a new home.

Associative memory, where the animal is triggered into "remembering" by some form of exterior stimulus—for example, a familiar voice—seems to be a different mechanism and one commonly seen when owners come to pick up their pet from the boarding kennel.

Powers of observation play an important part in both short-term and associative long-term canine memory. The reduction in normal brain function that accompanies such conditions as Canine Cognitive Dysfunction (CCD) in older dogs (see pages 180–181) significantly weakens all forms of the animal's memory. The tests in this section, if used regularly throughout your dog's life, particularly after the age of five or six years, will undoubtedly strengthen his memory.

Memory and observation score

It's now time to add up your dog's score for this section:

100 points or more Very intelligent.

80–99 points Above average.

50–79 points Average.

Less than 50 points Needs improvement, through regular repetition
and training (see pages 152–177).

Section E
Mental linkage tests

The ability to make mental connections is another quite
sophisticated component of intelligence in both humans and
dogs. It is part of the way in which your pet strings together
images and/or words to form a concept. This facility enables the
animal to get the idea.

Working with linkage

Dogs of any breed, including mutts, can be good at mental linkage, with
border collies, German shepherds, and spaniels in particular often
performing brilliantly. The best working border collies go about their
business by understanding the "language" of the shepherd, linking a large
number of words and visual signals in combination with the animal's own
interpretation of what is going on around him at every moment. Police
dogs, which are often German shepherds or spaniels, carry out their work
with similar skill.

The tests

To test for mental linkage in your dog, you must first have trained him in
basic behaviors such as "sit" (see pages 162–163). The tests in this section
should preferably be carried out indoors.

Older dogs

The thinking processes of older dogs often slow down when they reach
around 11 years of age onwards and they begin to perform mental
linkages less well.

35. Words and sounds

This simple test teaches your dog to understand that a sound substituted for a familiar word can be linked to a command for a particular action.

You will need:
• Your calm canine

What to do

1. With your dog in front of you and paying attention, clap your hands and then say "Sit." Repeat ten times.
2. Now clap your hands without giving the command. If your dog sits down, he has learned that a clap means the same as the command. If he does not sit down, repeat the procedure of clap followed by "Sit" a further ten times, then try the clap alone once more.

What's his score?

20 points if he makes the mental connection after only ten repetitions.

10 points if he makes the connection after 10–50 repetitions.

36. Words and signals

In this test you will be teaching your dog to link a visual signal to a command for an action. As with the previous test, any breed of dog can get the idea of this reasonably quickly.

You will need:

• Your calm canine

What to do

1. With your dog facing you, hold your clenched fist in front of his face.
2. Open and close your hand quickly and then say "Sit." Note how many repetitions it takes for your pet to obey the fist signal without it being accompanied by a verbal command.

What's his score?

20 points if he makes the mental connection after only ten repetitions.

10 points if he makes the connection after 10–50 repetitions.

Call it a day

If your dog has not made the mental connection between your sound or signal and the familiar word and action after 50 repetitions, stop the test and try again another day.

37. Words and scents

When choosing an aromatic substance to use for this test, take care: not only are canine senses more acute than ours, but some substances that are harmless to humans may be toxic to dogs. Examples of safe choices include toothpaste, shoe polish, a clove of garlic, fish paste, and rosewater.

You will need:
- Cottonwool buds
- A safe substance with a distinct aroma

What to do

1. Dip a cottonwool bud into the aromatic substance you have chosen, hold it in front of your dog's nose, and give the verbal command "Sit."
2. After several repetitions, substitute a clean cottonwool bud for the scented one. If your dog uses the bud as a visual clue and sits, stop for 30 seconds, and then repeat the test. He must learn that it's the smell that counts. Keep trying until your dog performs only in response to the smell.

What's his score?

20 points if he makes the mental connection after only ten repetitions.

10 points if he makes the connection after 10–50 repetitions.

Call it a day

If your dog has not made the mental connection between the smell and the familiar word and action after 50 repetitions, stop the test and try again another day.

Advanced training

If your dog is quick to get the idea in the tests given here and on pages 122–123, you may want to progress to using a variety of sound, visual, and scent clues for different behaviors. With perseverance (and luck), you will reach the point where your pet will sit when presented with a particular brand of perfume, lie down when you let him smell a wedge of ripe cheese, and come to you when you give a military salute!

Word linkage

Every dog, not just the famous Rico (see pages 112–113), has a vocabulary of words that he can understand, even though he obviously cannot say them. The bigger his vocabulary, the more developed his intelligence, so talk to your dog regularly and often. Always be consistent: use the same word every time for a particular behavior or object.

Consistency is key

When speaking to your dog, be clear and concise and take care not to puzzle him with alternative phrases. For example, when you mean "Come" don't say "I'm waiting" while patting your knee. Your voice must be friendly and smooth, never loud or harsh, and the pitch, tone, and volume should always be the same for the same command.

Complex commands

Once your dog understands a number of words, his intelligence can be enhanced significantly by putting some of them together to make a more complex request. For example, if he knows the meaning of "take," "slipper," and "Grandpa," he will soon catch on when told to "take the slipper to Grandpa." And if Grandpa has more than one pair of slippers, you may be able to progress to telling your dog to "take the black slippers to Grandpa," and then watch him select and deliver the correct footwear.

Linking ideas and events

Dogs are capable of linking two ideas in their mind, but they cannot associate events that are separated in time. If your dog runs off while you're on a walk, punishing him when he returns two hours later won't have the desired effect. Your dog will link the punishment with his return to you: he doesn't understand that the punishment is for failing to return two hours earlier.

38. Linking words

In this test we come much closer to your dog being able to link a number of words and understand their content. In other words, he is learning the grammar of your language, composed as it is of nouns, verbs, and adjectives. The proof of this is that your dog makes the correct response to your words.

You will need:

- Objects corresponding to the words you have chosen to use in the test

What to do

1. Teach your dog three or four words that can be linked together to make an instruction to act. Ideally, the words should include a verb like "bring" or "take," a noun or two like "sock," "toy," or "lead," an adjective such as a color (if you have a number of different-colored objects), and a family member's name or simply "me."

2. Now construct a basic sentence, such as "Bring the toy to me," and see if your dog can understand and act on it. The more words he can learn over time, the more interesting your "conversation" with him will become.

What's his score?

30 points if he correctly carries out an instruction containing four words from his vocabulary.

20 points if he correctly carries out an instruction containing three words from his vocabulary.

5 points if your dog correctly carries out an instruction containing two words from his vocabulary.

How did he do?

The tests given here and on pages 122–125 are some of the most important for evaluating the intelligence of your dog. It's now time to add up your dog's score for this section:

80 points or more Very intelligent.
75–79 points Above average.
60–74 Average.
Less than 60 points Needs improvement, through regular repetition and training (see pages 152–177).

Section F
Life experience tests

This final group of tests is different from the rest in that it involves you evaluating your pet's skills, training, and experience by answering a series of questions. There are no examination-type tests for your dog to perform, although each of the questions can be regarded as a "test."

Test instructions

All the questions that follow can be answered while you sit in your chair—you only have to *do* something in relation to one of them. Only you can answer them, because you know your dog so well.

Although this series of questions can be regarded as a mini-intelligence test in itself, it is best used as just a small part of your canine IQ tests. So, your dog's score for this section will be added to the total he has amassed so far.

39. Sound recognition

You are in the kitchen, with your dog in another room. Your start to unwrap some food within earshot of your pet. What does he do?

What's his score?

3 points if your dog comes into the kitchen as soon as he hears the sound, whether he is hungry or not.

1 point if he does not realize you are unwrapping food unless you do it in his presence.

40. Attention

Your dog wants to drink but his water bowl is empty. What does he do?

What's his score?

4 points if your dog draws your attention to the empty bowl in some way.

3 points if he comes to you and begins to whine.

2 points if he sits next to the bowl and whines.

1 point if he simply waits for you to notice the lack of water.

41. Coping with encounters

Out on a country walk with your dog, you meet a much larger dog, a cow, or a horse. How does your pet behave?

What's his score?

4 points if your dog sticks by you and does not engage the other animal in any way.

3 points if he growls or barks but only from a safe distance.

2 points if he approaches the animal cautiously or playfully.

0 points if he runs up to the animal, barking and harassing it, and perhaps even trying to give it a nip.

42. Playtime

You are playing with your dog and decide to stop, but he still wants to continue. How does he let you know?

What's his score?

3 points if your dog tries to start the game again.

2 points if he whines appealingly.

1 point if he growls.

43. Word recognition

Does your pet appear to recognize any of the following words: vet, walk, bed, food, (or the alternatives that are used in your household)? If so, how many?

What's his score?

1 point for each word your dog recognizes.

44. Determination

Out walking your dog, you come to a fence or wall that is too high for him to jump over. What does he do?

What's his score?

4 points if your dog runs along the fence looking for a way through.

2 points if he tries to burrow underneath the fence or waits for you to lift him over.

1 point if he loses interest and runs off in a different direction.

45. Road sense

Out walking your dog, you come to a busy road that you intend to cross. How does your dog react?

What's his score?

4 points if your dog stops on the pavement, clearly considering whether it's safe to cross.

3 points if he relies on you to make the decision that it's safe to cross.

1 point if he keeps on going and you are obliged to pull back on the lead.

46. People spotting

Does your dog appear to remember people who come to visit infrequently?

What's his score?

4 points if your dog always recognizes them.

3 points if he sometimes recognizes them.

2 points if he does not recognize them unless they gave him a food treat on previous visits.

0 points if he never recognizes them.

47. Noises

If your dog hears a strange noise outside when he is indoors, how does he react?

What's his score?

3 points if your dog clearly focuses on the source of the noise but remains quiet.

2 points if he barks and wants to go out to investigate.

1 point if he ignores the sound.

48. Somewhere new

When your pet finds himself in unfamiliar surroundings, how does he behave?

What's his score?

3 points if your dog is immediately curious and explores the place thoroughly.

2 points if he is fairly curious.

0 points if he is uninterested.

49. Contrition

You have caught your pet doing something naughty. How does he behave?

What's his score?

4 points if your dog slinks guiltily away, ears down and tail between his legs.

3 points if he cowers abjectly.

2 points if he dashes off looking worried.

1 point if he dashes off, eyes gleaming. No contrition there!

50. Mime game

Now, play this little charade. With your dog's full attention, pretend to reach for a piece of food and eat it. How does your pet react?

What's his score?

4 points if your dog clearly knows you are pretending.

3 points if he investigates the place from which you took the imaginary food to see if there is anything there.

2 points if he watches intently as you "eat."

1 point if he is totally uninterested.

How did he do?

It's now time to add up your dog's score for this section:

40 points and over Very intelligent.

30–39 points Above average.

20–29 points Average.

Fewer than 20 points Needs improvement, through regular repetition and training.

the test
results

Breed bonuses

You now need to add up your dog's scores for each section to obtain the total for the test series. Once you have done that, the next step is to add bonus points according to your dog's breed. Add them to the total and at last you have your dog's grand total score.

75 bonus points

Afghan hound
basset hound
bloodhound
bull terrier
bulldog
chow chow
Dandie Dinmont
Italian greyhound
Lakeland terrier
mastiff
Norfolk terrier
Old English sheepdog
Pekingese
petit basset griffon vendeen
Scottish terrier
Sealyham
shih tzu
Skye terrier
Tibetan terrier

50 bonus points

Akita
Australian shepherd dog
Bedlington terrier
bichon frise
black and tan coonhound
Boston terrier
boxer
Cavalier King Charles spaniel
dachshund
English and American
    foxhounds
English toy spaniel
Great Dane
greyhound
husky
Ibizan hound
Irish terrier
Irish wolfhound

Basset hound

Cavalier King Charles spaniel

malamute
otter hound
pointer (any except German
   shorthaired)
Rhodesian ridgeback
Saint Bernard
Scottish deerhound
Shar Pei
smooth- and wirehaired fox
   terriers
soft-coated wheaten terrier
Staffordshire bull terrier
Tibetan spaniel
Welsh terrier
West Highland terrier

30 bonus points

affen- and miniature
   pinschers
Airedale
American Staffordshire terrier
Australian cattle dog
Australian terrier
bearded collie
Belgian sheepdog
Belgian tervueren
Bernese mountain dog
border collie
border terrier
Bouvier des Flandres
cairn terrier

corgi
dalmatian
Doberman
elkhound
German shepherd
German shorthaired pointer
golden and Labrador
   retrievers
keeshond
Kerry blue terrier
Malinois
Manchester terrier
Newfoundland
Norwich terrier
papillon
Pomeranian
poodle
rottweiler
Samoyed
schipperke
schnauzers
Shetland sheepdog
Silky terrier
Yorkshire terrier
all other spaniels and
   retrievers
mutts
unlisted breeds

How did he do?

So, what do you think you've got? A Caninestein perhaps? Whatever his score, you can be sure that your dog is far from dumb. As with people, so with dogs: many of the most attractive, valuable, and remarkable individuals are definitely not among the intelligentsia. Character is what counts—and all dogs have plenty of that.

Grand total score, including breed bonus

483–503 points Yours is a Top Dog!

462–482 points An Oscar winner among dogs.

441–461 points Definitely playing in the canine mental Olympics.

Less than 440 points Must try harder—keep on training and testing.

Improving his score

Above all, remember to treat all the tests as fun. Also bear in mind that your dog's score can be improved through additional training (see pages 152–177). A keen dog trainer friend of mine put his border terrier through the series of tests in this book and scored a very mediocre 395 at the first attempt. After more training and lots of practice in the various tests, the little dog went on to score a highly respectable 445 at his retest!

canine
crammer
college

Back to school

If your pet's total score in his first series of tests was mediocre, or even downright disappointing, it's now time to set about improving his performance before you embark on a repeat series. Yes, it's back to school!

Keys to success

Training really can improve your dog's intelligence. Successful teaching of your pet depends on you communicating what you want him to do clearly and consistently, and the dog then understanding this and responding obediently. This trio of communication, comprehension, and obedience is as vital in the education of dogs as it is in children.

Top training tips

- Keep talking to your pet, whether you are training him or not.
- As with visual signals, be consistent in always using the same word for the same behavior. Learn which pitch and tone of voice work best for each behavior during training.
- Link your words to your body language: for example, demonstrate what "sit" means by sitting down in a relaxed fashion next to your dog a number of times and in different locations.
- Whenever you are communicating with your dog, the sound of your voice should be cheerful and even.
- Never shout: dogs have acute hearing and listen more intently when you speak softly.
- During play periods, use praise abundantly so that your pet comes to value it as a reward during training sessions.

Breed mentality

Improving your dog's intelligence through training depends partly on what breed or mixture of breeds he is. If he is a mutt, decide what type he is—for example, terrier or pastoral dog. Then concentrate on the types of training recommended over the following pages for the canine family or families to which your pet wholly or partly belongs.

Hounds

Hounds in general do not rank highly in the canine league table for intelligence. The most intelligent is the Norwegian elkhound. Hounds have a strong tendency to become distracted, in the case of the scent hounds by a passing smell and for sight hounds by some peripheral activity. They must learn to pay attention and concentrate on commands so that they can begin to understand them. You have to keep on top of their training, repeatedly testing them with the important "sit," "stay," "come," and "fetch" commands (see pages 162–165, 168–169 and 174–176). Ensure good eye contact between you and your dog at all times so that he is focused intently on you and the job in hand.

Beagle

Pastoral dogs

Some of the most intelligent breeds of dog are included in this group, which covers various collies and sheepdogs, corgis and the Samoyed, among others. If you want to improve on this, concentrate on problem-solving tests and games such as the Outdoor and Advanced Treasure Hunts and the Indoor Treasure Hunts (see pages 84–91 and 108–111).

Old English sheepdog

Airedale terrier

Terriers

Ten terrier breeds are found in the "above average" rankings for intelligence. These busy little creatures have a tendency to be undisciplined and easily distracted, and one of the most difficult to train is that giant among them, the Airedale. Your terrier's IQ can be improved by you emphasizing obedience to commands and insisting on your dog ignoring distractions while training.

Bulldog

Utility dogs

Utility dogs vary greatly in intelligence. While the poodle is believed to be the second most intelligent dog of all, the chow chow and bulldog are among the four least intelligent breeds. The best training for this group involves the Houdini Hound, Canny Canine, Treat under Towel and Hide-and-Seek tests (see pages 52–53, 66–69 and 96–97).

Working dogs

It is crucial and only fair to consider the IQ of the breeds in this group—which include the Doberman, boxer, Great Dane, and Saint Bernard—in relation to the jobs they were bred to do. Their brainpower is focused mainly on one particular field of activity. Playing games with these dogs that enable them to bring out the natural physical and mental abilities of their breed can enhance their intelligence. For some, their predominant talent lies in some form of visual skill or in thought, as in problem solving. However, it is best not to engage in rougher games such as wrestling or tug-of-war with them as their generally dominant nature may release a tendency towards aggression.

Bernese mountain dog

Papillon

Toy dogs

These small breeds vary in their level of intelligence, but do not assume
that small size means small IQ in a pea-sized brain! Some toy dogs score
very highly in intelligence tests, and the papillon and Pomeranian rank as
two of the brightest breeds. The intelligence of this group can be
significantly improved by games and tests of thought and skill such as
Words and Sounds, Words and Signals, Words and Scents, and Linking
Words (see pages 122–125 and 128–129).

Pointer

Sporting/gundogs

Every one of the 30-plus breeds in this group—which includes all the spaniels, pointers, and retrievers, as well as the Weimaraner and vizsla—is very intelligent and none falls anywhere near the bottom half of the canine IQ rankings. By nature they are sharp, focused, and highly obedient—they have to be, in their work as hunters' assistants. As you might expect, these dogs' intelligence can best be promoted by tests and games that involve their innate physical abilities of searching and tracking by sight or scent, such as Tracking and Treasure Hunts (see pages 62–63 and 84–91).

150   Canine crammer college

Mutts

The principle of hybrid vigor ensures that mutts tend to be at least as intelligent as their pedigree relations, if not more so. On average, mutts possess bigger brains than pedigrees: this is either because of genetic expression of that hybrid vigor, or because the more interesting experiences these dogs tend to have from puppyhood onwards, as compared to pampered show-bench types, stimulate the brain literally to grow bigger.

To increase the intelligence of your mutt, you need to play games and set tests that draw out the innate characteristics of the breeds in his makeup. For example, for pastoral and gundog types, that means problem solving; for terrier types, obedience training; for hound types, reinforcing their ability to concentrate. Whatever the mixture that is your pet, training him to respond promptly and reliably to voice or visual commands is vital and should be kept up.

improving IQ through training

Advice for training

Improvement through training involves you and your dog
regularly repeating the tests and playing games together.
Practice *does* make perfect! Games and tests like the Treasure
Hunts and Hide-and-Seek (see pages 84–91, 96–97, and 108–111)
will hone your dog's natural abilities, but it is essential that your
pet also has a basis of trained behavior: in particular, that he is
attentive, responsive to your commands, and very obedient.

Do-it-yourself

Training does take time, and while you may prefer to go to dog training
classes or engage a professional dog trainer, most owners will find that the
training techniques presented here are easy and interesting, and produce
remarkable results.

Reward and reinforcement

Training should be by reward and *never* by physical punishment. Rewards that are given in the form of food treats, praise, or a pat on the head after your dog behaves correctly are known as "positive reinforcement." "Negative reinforcement" is a stimulus that the dog dislikes and which is withdrawn when he performs correctly.

Another form of reinforcement often employed in dog training is "secondary reinforcement." This is used where it is not possible or appropriate to reward a correct behavior at the proper time. A sound from a small hand-held clicker device tells the dog that he has performed correctly and that a reward will follow in due course. Naturally, you should never forget to do this.

Training principles

Before you begin training your dog, you need to understand some basic facts and principles:

- Be patient and *never* lose your temper.
- Work with your dog regularly, preferably every day.
- Puppies can begin training at three to four months of age; old dogs take longer to train.
- Training sessions should last no longer than 10 minutes for puppies and 20 minutes for adult dogs. The first sessions should last only 5 minutes but can be repeated several times daily for the first few days.
- Begin using verbal commands when training, but accompany them with some sort of visual cue: a gesture with a finger, hand, or arm, or a nod of your head. Eventually you will be able to drop the verbal commands altogether and use the visual signals alone.
- Use a collar and lead to help you train until you have complete verbal control.
- Do not be too lavish with food rewards: give pea-sized pieces together with plenty of praise. Do not give chocolate: it contains theobromine, which is toxic for dogs and in particular toy breeds. Grapes and raisins are also toxic for dogs and should not be used as a reward.

Essential foundations

The basic behaviors you should teach your dog to enable him to perform far better in the IQ tests and games are:

- Walk to heel
- Watch
- Sit
- Lie down
- Stay
- Come
- Fetch

We are not concerned here with more advanced training for party tricks like shaking hands and taking a bow, but if you and your pet get great enjoyment from your training, you can certainly move on to these in the future.

Watch

In the IQ tests, I frequently mention the need for your pet to pay attention. The "watch" command enables you to gain your dog's attention, and consequently is the best exercise with which to begin each training session.

What to do

1 Hold a treat near to your face, call your dog's name, and add the word "watch," until he looks at you. Make sure he knows it is a treat you are showing him—if necessary, bring it close to his face for a second or two, then take it away and hold it high.

Vision problems
Understandably, older dogs with the beginnings of degenerative changes in the lens or retina of their eyes may not perform reliably on the "watch" command. This is often the first indication of a pet's failing vision to be noticed by the owner.

2 Stay in this position for a few seconds with your dog paying attention. He may even sit for you, but don't worry if he doesn't—the important thing is to hold his attention. If he remains focused on you for a few seconds, give him the treat and praise him so that he knows you are pleased.

3 Repeat steps 1 and 2 but wait longer before rewarding your dog if he remains focused. If he looks away or loses interest, hide the treat behind your back until he looks up at you, wondering what happened to the treat, and then reward him. When he performs reliably you can drop the "watch" command but continue using his name.

Walking to heel

Teaching your dog to walk to heel is the first requirement. When you set out to perform some of the tests, play games, or simply go for a walk, your pet should be close by you until you give him permission to run free.

What to do

1 Have your dog on a lead that you hold firmly. Shorten the lead and bring him into the required position, with his right shoulder beside your left leg.

2 Say "Heel" firmly and begin walking. Continue with reassuring words of praise to give your dog reassurance. If he pulls forward or hangs back, tug very gently on the lead as you change your walking direction to put him back in position.

3 Carefully begin to practice turns, initially only to your right, away from your dog. Turning left can panic him at first as he may become entangled with your legs. Once your dog is fully used to walking to heel on the lead, you can introduce the left turn.

4 When your dog walks and turns in both directions reliably with the lead remaining slack, progress to walking to heel without the lead, again in a quiet place at first.

Where to train

Your first "heel" training sessions should take place in a quiet spot such as your garden, a park or open land. Only after your dog is doing well there should you take him out on the streets:

- Don't stop to talk to people.
- Don't avoid other dogs, but if you meet them keep walking.
- Don't allow lamp-post sniffing.
- Don't go out among traffic and crowds too soon.

Sit

Now is a good time to proceed to training the "sit" command that is used in some of the intelligence tests in this book. Use it routinely at other times before giving your dog something he wants, such as a toy or a walk outside.

What to do

1 Hold a small food treat in front of your dog's nose as he stands facing you.

Sitting options

Watch your dog when he sits. How does he do it? Dogs use two different ways to sit down from a standing position. Smaller and medium-sized breeds usually keep their front legs still while bringing their hind legs forward beneath their stomach to meet their front paws. Bigger dogs do the reverse and keep their hind legs still, draw their front feet back to meet their hind feet and simultaneously drop their bottom to the ground.

Caution

It is important that dogs with hip joint problems such as dysplasia, Legge Perthes disease, or arthritis are not asked to sit for long periods of time during training.

2 Move the treat slowly and steadily up and over his head. Your dog's nose will almost certainly follow the lure upward and backward, while his rear end descends to the floor and into the sit position.

3 As his bottom lands on the floor, say "Sit" and give him the treat. Be careful not to hold the treat too high above his head or he may jump for it instead of sitting. After several repetitions, you should find that simply sweeping your hand upwards without a treat will produce the sit response.

Stay

Once your dog has mastered the sit and will do it on command, it is time to introduce "stay" and then "sit-stay." It's a good idea to spend a few minutes on training this behavior each time you take your pet out for a walk.

What to do

1 Walk with your dog to heel and on the lead, then command him to "Sit."

2 Now command him to "Stay" and reinforce with a visual signal by extending one arm away from your body, palm upward. For your dog, psychologically, this lessens the gap between you. Walk one step away from him, still with your hand held out. If the dog moves to come to you, stop the exercise and return close to him. If he stays, reward him and move on to Step 3.

3 Move two steps away from the dog. Keep your hand held out, saying "Stay."

4 Now move on to the "sit-stay" command without a lead, gradually increasing your distance from the dog. You can develop the command by turning your back to your dog and also going further away until you are out of sight. When you return, praise your dog for his obedience and walk on.

Down

It will now be easy for you to move on to training your dog to lie down, which is a natural extension of the sit. Obviously, all breeds are capable of this behavior, but the toy dogs are the easiest and quickest to train in it, as they are light, nimble, and close to the ground.

What to do

1 Begin with your dog on a smooth but not too slippery surface rather than a carpet or rug. Tell him to sit and then show him a food treat.

2 Move the treat down from in front of his nose to the floor immediately in front of his forepaws. If the treat is too far from him he may be tempted to stand and walk to it.

3 As he begins to ease himself down onto the floor, say "Lie down" and give him the treat as a reward. Give praise if he then maintains the lying position, but not if he gets up.

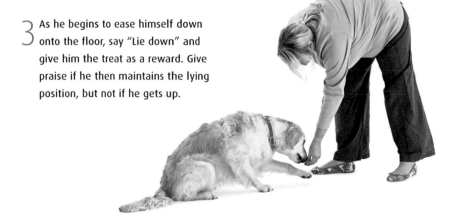

Come

Next on the list is the "come" command, one of the most important for insisting on obedience during training, testing, and everyday life. It enables you to keep close control of your dog, particularly outdoors if it looks like trouble might be brewing or you are both about to do something potentially dangerous like cross a road. The training is best carried out using a long, extendable lead.

What to do

1 Tell your dog to sit. When he does, turn and walk away from him.

2 Once you are a few yards away, turn and call your dog by name and say "Come" emphatically. If he hesitates, tug the lead gently and take up the slack as he moves toward you.

3 Keep calling and praising him as he comes toward you. When he arrives, reward him with praise and a food treat.

4 When you think your dog is ready, dispense with the lead. During the off-lead training, you can try turning away as you give the command. This plays on your dog's pack instinct to follow his leader. If subsequently he refuses to come or sits just out of range, go back to lead training. Do not scold your pet if he does not come to you on the odd occasion. Instead, lavish praise on him when he does!

Take and give

The "fetch" command is involved in several of the IQ tests, as well as some of the best games you can play with your dog. It has four component behaviors that you will need to teach first, especially if your dog is older. These are "take," "give," "hold," and "drop" (see pages 172–173). "Take" and "drop" can take quite a while to train—in some cases, a few weeks. You will need patience.

What to do

1 Put your dog in the sit position beside your left leg. Gently open his mouth by putting the palm of your left hand under his lower jaw and inserting your thumb behind his canine (fang) tooth.

2 When your dog's mouth is open, place the object between his teeth with your right hand and say "Take." Then close his mouth by clasping it gently with your right hand.

3 Give your pet lots of praise. Say "Give" and at once take the object out of his mouth. Give more praise and a food reward. You will achieve rapid results by repeating the sequence six to ten times during each training session.

"Fetch" toys

You can use a ball for this training, but something with a horizontal dimension like a rubber or plastic dumbbell is preferable. The easier it is for your dog to pick up the object neatly, the better the training will go. Some trainers use a short (6-inch) length of smooth tree branch or firewood. You must ensure there are no spikes or splinters that could harm your pet, so it is probably safest to avoid these options. Best of all is an object that is already one of your dog's favorite playthings.

Hold and drop

The training for "hold" and "drop" begins in the same way as for "take" and "give" (see pages 170–171), but now he needs to learn to hold on to the object for longer and then release it on your command.

What to do

1 With your dog in the sit position by your left leg, gently open his mouth by putting the palm of your left hand under his lower jaw and inserting your thumb behind his canine (fang) tooth.

2 When your dog's mouth is open, put the object in between his teeth with your right hand and say "Take." Close his mouth by clasping it gently with your right hand. Hold it closed and say "Hold."

3 Praise your dog while he does this and then, after only a second or two, release your right hand and say "Drop." Give praise and a food treat as soon as he drops the object. Repeat the sequence two or three times, while keeping your dog's mouth closed for several seconds longer each time. When your dog has reached the point where he will reliably take, hold, and drop, continue the exercise while gradually lowering the object each time he takes it correctly, until he will pick it up from the floor at his feet.

Fetch

The "fetch" command can be quite difficult to train if your dog does not belong to one of the naturally retrieving breeds, and particularly if he is short-nosed. Use a toy such as a ball, dumbbell, or bone made from plastic. Do not use pieces of tree branch, which may carry spikes or splinters that could injure your dog's mouth. If possible, begin training your pet as a puppy: nothing delights a pup more than running after and retrieving balls and other toys.

Training a puppy to fetch

1 When your pup voluntarily retrieves an object and proudly brings it back to you, praise his skill and enthusiasm abundantly but do not wrench it from his mouth—he must lay it down or drop it in front of you. He will soon learn that you will not throw the object again unless he gives it up.

2 Now, throw an object and say "Fetch." When he returns, say "Good boy" and then "Drop" as he lets it go. Pick up the object and give him more praise.

3 Once your puppy has grasped the idea, say "Fetch" together with the name of an object: for example, "Fetch the ball." Begin to use two or three different objects in the game, say a ball, a toy, and a plastic bone. This way, he will soon begin to learn the names of objects and how to discriminate between them. You never know, one day he might turn out to be smarter than the famous Rico (see pages 112–113)!

Training an older dog to fetch

An older dog should be trained to "take," "give," "hold," and "drop" (see pages 170–173) before you move on to teaching him to "fetch."

1 When your dog will reliably pick up an object from the floor at his feet (see pages 172–173), place it progressively further away: 1 foot, 3 feet, and then 6 feet. Repeat no more than six times in a session to avoid boring him.

2 Now throw the object a short distance and say "Fetch." Give praise when he picks it up. When he brings it back to you, say "Give" and reward with more praise and a food treat. If he fools around or runs off with the object, give the "come" command (see pages 168–169) as soon as he picks up the object, and give him praise and a treat when he obeys by returning to you. Gradually increase the throwing distance and, if you wish, introduce the "sit" and "hold" commands (see pages 162–163 and 172–173) when he gets back.

Natural talents

As you might expect, the gundog breeds have a natural talent for learning these behaviors quickly while toy dogs, particularly short-nosed types, can find them more difficult. For training such pets you should use an object that is not too heavy, fits neatly into their small jaws, and is shaped so as to be easy to pick up. Some dogs will carry anything no matter what material it is made from, while others will pick up only soft or rubber toys. Take account of any such preferences in your pet when starting his training.

other ways
to improve
your dog's IQ

Health and IQ

For tip-top mental function, your dog must be physically healthy.
There are a number of different aspects of his health that may
affect his performance in IQ tests, quite apart from the
consequences for his overall quality of life.

Conditions affecting IQ

- Obesity not only makes movement during exercise and testing less easy,
  but may also reduce the activity of your dog's brain cells. If your pet is
  overweight, your vet can advise on a safe slimming diet.
- Hormonal upsets such as hypothyroidism can have similar effects on the
  canine brain.
- Most common of all in reducing a dog's capacity to train, test, or play
  well are conditions affecting the heart and problems with the skeletal
  system such as hip dysplasia, patella luxation (displacement of the
  kneecap), and arthritis. All these conditions need investigation and
  treatment by a vet.

Canine Cognitive Dysfunction (CCD)

In dogs over eight years old, the canine equivalent of Alzheimer's Disease
is now well recognized. The pathological changes in the animal's brain are
very similar to those found in human patients. These changes cause
deterioration in the way a dog thinks, learns, and remembers, and so lead
to an apparent drop in intelligence. Accompanying symptoms include a
tendency to get lost in familiar situations, lack of response to his name or
familiar commands, aimless wandering, inability to recognize family
members, and unwillingness to play, go for walks, or even step outside.
Unfortunately, currently there is no cure for CCD, but a prescribed drug
called selegiline may be effective in improving your dog's quality of life.

If your dog is diagnosed with CCD, you can help to control the condition by providing a diet rich in antioxidants (found in fruit and vegetables) and giving regular moderate exercise, short and gentle play sessions, and simple, compassionate commands—and, above all, by displaying infinite patience.

Diet and IQ

Is there such a thing as canine brain food? Can your dog's dinner affect his intelligence? There is much talk nowadays about how certain foods, vitamins, and other supplements may improve children's intelligence and their performance at school, and the same applies to your dog.

Dietary deficiencies

A good, balanced diet is essential for your dog's overall health. Just as a dog that doesn't feel fit or endures chronic aches and pains will understandably be lacking in enthusiasm for training and tests, so too his brain and his senses of vision and hearing—all vital in demonstrating powers of intelligence—can be adversely affected by deficiencies in his diet.

Brain foods

The most influential brain foods are the fatty acids: omega 3, found in oily fish, and omega 6, found in plant oils and in pork and poultry fat. These chemicals are essential for perfect brain function. Making sure that your dog's diet contains adequate fatty acids is important if

he is to attain his optimum IQ, but be warned—overdosing by enthusiastic owners can cause problems, particularly of the liver and circulatory system.

Using supplements

Other chemicals that play an important role in keeping nerve cells healthy and maintaining the supply of plenty of oxygenated blood to the brain are the food supplements choline, inositol, and B vitamins. These, plus ginkgo biloba, a herbal product that the Chinese have used since time immemorial to maintain memory, can be obtained in capsule or tablet form from health food stores and are generally regarded as safe for dogs. Nevertheless, it is always a good idea to discuss your pet's dietary requirements with your vet before giving him a supplement of any kind. Giving pills as dietary supplements is essentially "artificial" and can be expensive. A truly balanced canine diet avoids the need for such things. Your vet can advise you on this.

training and test schedule

Training schedule

If possible, you should first take your dog through the complete set of IQ tests. This will give you a baseline score on which he will improve through repetition and training.

Training guidelines

- Even if your dog is already trained in obedience behaviors like "sit," "stay," and "fetch," you should keep refreshing them throughout the test series. If he isn't, obedience training is the key area in which you must begin (see pages 152–177).
- If you cannot follow through the whole test series continuously, try to complete a section or two and note the scores achieved until you can carry on with the rest of the tests.
- Do some tests and training with your dog each day.

Week 1

Obedience training/refreshing
Houdini hound (pages 52–53)
Packet puzzler (pages 54–55)
Find the food (pages 64–65)
Canny canine (pages 66–67)
Treat under towel (pages 68–69)
Outdoor treasure hunts 1 and 2
(pages 84–87)

Cup and treat (page 102)
Indoor treasure hunts 1 and 2
(pages 108–111)
Repetition of any tests that were
weak on initial testing

Week 2

Obedience training/refreshing
Peek-a-boo 1 and 2 (pages 56–57)
Mini maze (pages 60–61)
Treat and fence (pages 70–71)
Hide-and-seek (pages 96–97)
Smiley face (pages 100–101)
Repetition of any tests that were
   weak on initial testing

Week 3

Obedience training/refreshing
Mega maze (pages 58–59)
Canine accountancy (pages 76–77)
Obstacle course (pages 92–95)
Life experience tests (pages 130–135)
Repetition of any tests that were
   weak on initial testing

Week 4

Obedience training/refreshing
New toy (page 103)
Rico's tests 1, 2, and 3 (pages 112–113)
Find the treat 1 and 2 (pages 114–115)
Spot the difference 1 and 2
   (pages 116–117)
Repetition of any tests that were weak
   on initial testing

Week 5

Obedience training/refreshing
Tracking (pages 62–63)
Advanced treasure hunts 1–4 (pages 88–91)
Rico's tests 1, 2, and 3 (pages 112–113)
Repetition of any tests that were
   weak on initial testing

Week 6

Obedience training/refreshing
New words (pages 98–99)
Smiley face (pages 100–101)
Rico's tests 1, 2, and 3 (pages 112 113)
Words and sounds (page 122)
Words and signals (page 123)
Words and scents (pages 124–125)
Linking words (pages 128–129)
Repetition of any tests that were
   weak on initial testing

Week 7

Complete the test series again for your
   dog's new grand total score

Index

Acknowledgments

While writing this book I have received invaluable advice from my editors, Trevor Davies and Kerenza Swift, and all the team at Hamlyn, and also from the indefatigable Sarah Widdecombe. Professor Stanley Coren most kindly gave me permission to quote from his seminal book on canine intelligence, *The Intelligence of Dogs*. My sister, Vivienne, kept me going throughout with innumerable coffees and toasted bacon sandwiches.

Picture credits

Commissioned photography © **Octopus Publishing Group Limited**/Russell Sadur apart from the following: **Alamy** Glow Images 71. **istockphoto.com** Boris Shapiro 34. **Octopus Publishing Group Limited** 161; / Angus Murray 22, 37, 176; /Russell Sadur 7, 10, 11, 11, 12, 13, 14, 15, 16, 17, 18, 28, 29, 30, 31, 33, 36, 39, 44, 45, 48, 55, 69, 72, 73, 77, 81, 85, 87, 88, 89, 90, 91, 93, 95, 101, 102, 104, 108, 111, 113, 113, 114, 116, 119, 122, 123, 125, 131, 133, 141, 143, 144, 151, 154, 155, 156, 157, 158, 159, 160, 161, 162, 163, 164, 165, 166, 167, 168, 169, 170, 171, 172, 177, 181, 182, 184; /Steve Gorton 23, 26, 103, 134, 174. **Shutterstock** Vera Shushmarkina 79.

Executive editor Trevor Davies
Editor Kerenza Swift
Executive art editor Mark Stevens
Designer Peter Gerrish
Production controller Carolin Stransky